# The Return of the Legend

## Triumph

David Minton

CHARTWELL
BOOKS, INC.

A QUINTET BOOK

Published by Chartwell Books
A Division of Book Sales, Inc.
PO box 7100
Edison, New Jersey 08818-7100

This edition produced for sale in the U.S.A.,
its territories and dependencies only.

ISBN 0-7858-0309-2

This book was designed and produced by
Quintet Publishing Limited
6 Blundell Street
London N7 9BH

Creative Director: Richard Dewing
Designers: Neal Cobourne and Wendy Bartlet
Project Editor: Stefanie Foster
Editor: Kit Coppard

Typeset in Great Britain by
Central Southern Typesetters, Eastbourne
Manufactured by
Regent Publishing Services Ltd, Singapore
Printed by Leefung Asco Printers Ltd, China

AUTHOR'S ACKNOWLEDGEMENTS
I would especially like to thank the following individuals
for their help. Few truisms hold greater veracity than the
popular, "Those who can, do, and those who can't
write/teach/criticise (as you wish)". These good folk
"do": Colin Missen, Brian Bennet, John Anderson,
Bob Bufton and Dan Force. Each man is an expert in
Triumphs of a particular era. All are of the calloused
thumb variety. Many thanks too to Chris Skellern, of
Skellern's Triumph agency in Worcester for his generous
loan of new Triumphs. Also to his service department
staff's enlightening knowledge. Lastly, thanks to Ricardo
Consulting Engineers for its invaluable assistance.

Quintet Publishing would like to extend thanks to
Triumph Motorcycles, Hinckley, for permission to
use the Triumph logo and for supplying pictures
of new Triumphs. Triumph Motorcycles Limited bears no
responsibility for the content of this book, having had no
part in its origination or preparation.

*"Force . . . speeds in fury to its undoing and continues to modify
according to the occasion. Always lives ill at ease with whoever
holds it. It grows slowly from small beginnings and makes itself a
terrible and marvellous power. Force is only the desire of flight."*
LEONARDO DA VINCI, FLORENCE, SIXTEENTH CENTURY

# Contents

# INTRODUCTION

To be great needs not to be good as well. Triumph is a great name in motorcycling – debatably the greatest – but for its most devoted enthusiasts to assume that all its products are good reduces the brand to blandness. Triumph is great because, above and beyond any other make, it has changed the (motorcycle) world and, against all odds, has endured. Its only historical rival is Harley-Davidson which, like Triumph, was founded immediately after the turn of the century. Unlike H.D., however, Triumph has twice changed the world of motorcycling profoundly. The first occasion was immediately prior to World War II, when the Speed Twin shook the motorcycle industry to its foundations and set a design lead that was to last for half a century. And the second came in the wake of the same hostilities, when young America, worldly at last and eager for whatever was on offer, took the Triumph twin to its rich and rewarding bosom. This it did so

enthusiastically that the popularity of the agile silver-blue British motorbikes not only caused Harley-Davidson more grief than even the Indian motorcycles had, it awoke the export ambitions of Soichiro Honda. Thereafter, things were never quite the same again. "You meet the nicest people on a . . .".

This book is unashamedly romantic, for it tells a story of great endeavor and high ideals, power and speed and devotion to a cause far beyond that of normal commercial duty. Say the name "Turner" to any dedicated motorcyclist and he or she will, if they be of any experience, acknowledge that the conversation is close to the source of virtue itself. But should we, us motorcyclists, couple with Turner, Schulte, then Page, McCormack, and Bloor?

We have concentrated on the motorcycles themselves, for they are the real heroes of the story. You will not, however, find between these pages a nut-by-bolt account of development minutiae or chronological frame numbering: they

are the subject of other fine books. And you won't find every Triumph model ever made. Our aim is to take you on an exciting armchair ride through the world's oldest and greatest motorcycle maker via its significant motorcycles, events, and people.

Unlike most other books on the subject, this one does not make the erroneous assumption that real Triumph history began post-World War II with the surviving Speed Twin. British history did not begin with the Norman Conquest of 1066 nor American history with the arrival of the Pilgrim Fathers in 1620. We, then, shall start at the proper place – the beginning. Don't make the error of assuming, as so many modern riders do, that old means slow and boring. Anyone who has wrestled with a 1921 wayward "Riccy" at 65mph (105km/h) will appreciate all too well the need for high-speed courage even in the old days.

Enjoy your "ride"!

◀ The start of one of the great desert races of California, circa the 1970s and now, alas, almost defunct.

◀ The Triumph Speed Triple, the 900cc café race out of Hinckley.

## FROM THE FIRST TO THE LAST

*I*t is, perhaps, entirely right and proper that Triumph, the most quintessentially British motorcycle, has such a cosmopolitan history. The

company was founded by a German and its engineering origins are German, while its more recent post-WW2 global success was largely US-inspired. Only now can the new Triumph company be said to be wholly British, although ironically with a type of engine that is rightly accepted as typically Japanese. The most remarkable part of Triumph's long history lies not in its past, but in its present, and much less astonishing than the brand's continuance is its actual resurrection. That the greatest of the old British factories should rise above its former rivals thankfully defies the pattern of history.

THE NEWCOMER TO motorcycling history may be surprised to learn of the German origins of two of Britain's most highly respected motorcycle manufacturers. Veloce (Velocette) was founded in 1905 by the Gutgemann (anglicized to "Goodman") family, and then there was Triumph in 1903. Given historical perspective, perhaps it is not so strange. The European industrial revolution of the 19th century began in Britain, largely as a consequence of the surplus wealth generated by its global trading being employed to fund research and development of the new hot-metal industries. Thus, Britain in the late 19th century occupied a position similar to that enjoyed by the United States in the late 20th: it had become a welcoming magnet to people with technical skills, energy, and ambition.

In 1884 Siegfried Betteman left the Bavarian city of Nuremberg to make his fortune in London, then the rich and rewarding heart of world trade. He was a well-educated, intelligent young man who recognized the potential opportunities awaiting commercial investment in the astonishing bicycle craze of the final years of the century. More than any other single device, the bicycle, so simple to make, so cheap to own, yet so joyously rewarding to use, changed the social fabric of Britain. Ordinary men and women began to discover the heady delights of personal freedom brought by personal transportation. The bicycle set the scene for the motorcycle, and Betteman set the scene for his own business. He named it Triumph because the word's meaning is recognized in most European languages.

By 1887 his bicycle company was flourishing enough for its proprietor to take on an assistant, Mauritz Schulte, another young German. Unlike the commercially astute Betteman, Schulte was a talented engineer, and within twelve months he had convinced his employer of the need to turn from being merely a commercial parts assembler

to becoming a true manufacturer. They moved from London and, with a capital investment of £150 each, plus an additional, and ultimately significant, £500 sum from Betteman's parents, entered into partnership as a manufacturer of unusually high-quality bicycles in Coventry.

## The first Triumphs

By 1895 Schulte had, by the standards of the day, become an experienced motorcyclist following his methodical study, and rejection, of the design of the Hildebrand and Wolfmüller motorcycle from Germany. He was the archetypal engineer – ambitious yet patient – and over the following six years became increasingly dissatisfied with the

▲ DESIGNED SPECIFICALLY FOR WOMEN, THE 1914-25 225CC TWO-STROKE "BABY" TRIUMPH HAD A TWO-SPEED TRANSMISSION AND WAS PADDLE-STARTED BY THE SEATED RIDER. ITS TOP-GEAR SPEED RANGE WAS 3-35MPH (5-56KM/H). IT WAS IMMENSELY POPULAR IN THE OLD BRITISH COLONIES AND IN EUROPE, AND IT SOLD IN THOUSANDS. DEALERS ORDERED IT IN LATINIZED TELEGRAPHIC CODE FOR ACCURACY: 1 – "BABY", 2 – "DUO", 3 – "TRES", 6 "SEI", 9 – "NOVE", 12 – "DOCE", 15 – "KINCE", 20 – "VENTI".

commercial engines then available. In 1902 a Minerva-engined Triumph was produced, and the following year it incorporated Triumph's (Schulte's) own improved Minerva engine. Far from satisfied with the results, Triumph then turned to J. A. Prestwich (JAP), which was then in its first year of production, with similar consequences. During what must have been very trying times, Schulte nevertheless committed himself to his goal, and finally in 1905 produced his company's first completely in-house motorcycle, the historic 3HP (300 cc) model.

## The industrial story

Betteman was an ambitious man and quickly became a major force in local politics. He was elected Mayor of Coventry in 1913, by which time he had joined the social circles of the British political establishment. During World War I, Triumph became a major player in the transportation field when it was contracted to supply British and Allied forces with 30,000 Model H machines. After the war Betteman's ambition to drop bicycle manufacturing in favor of cars conflicted with Schulte's preference for two-wheeler specialization. By this time Betteman had the backing of a new and powerful adviser, Colonel Sir Claude Holbrook, the man who had contracted Triumph to supply the army with its motorcycles, and Schulte was forced to retire with a £15,000 bonus.

The car division had barely started operations when the Depression arrived. The company survived only by splitting up, under the advice of its banker, Lloyds. The motorcycle division was purchased by Jack Sangster, the dynamic and astute brains behind Ariel, which he had obtained in 1932. Reluctant to disturb Triumph's delicately balanced manufacturing and distributing operations, Sangster appeared to leave well enough alone by "promoting" Betteman to become Triumph's chairman — in practice, a largely

▲ HOPE SPRINGS ETERNAL, HOWEVER MISGUIDEDLY. DESPITE THEIR UNDOUBTED QUALITY, THE 175CC (BSA BANTAM ENGINE) AND 250CC SURPRISINGLY POWERFUL TWIN CYLINDER OHV FOUR-STROKE VERSIONS OF THE BSA SUNBEAM AND TRIUMPH TIGRESS SCOOTERS — ARRIVED AS THE 1950S SCOOTER BOOM WAS WANING, AND FAILED.

honorific position lacking executive power. By 1933, Val Page had been brought in to design a desperately needed new line of machines; but then in 1936 Sangster installed Edward Turner as general manager and chief designer. Page had been chief designer, and Turner's boss, at Ariel. Page left Triumph for BSA as Turner came in. Thenceforward, Triumph's design policy changed from one of almost Germanic idealism to that of commercial expediency. The former policy had lifted the company to a position of highly respected eminence until the Depression got under way. The company was now about to enter

a second period of equal success, although for reasons so different they would influence the entire motorcycling world.

After consolidating Triumph's position by reducing a multimodel line to its bare essentials and then modernizing them into what became the 1936/39 Tigers 70, 80, and 90, Turner designed the Speed Twin. The man was a near genius of commercial opportunism rather than of design originality. He used his knowledge of parallel-twin characteristics gained with his design and protracted development of the Ariel Square Four (two gear-coupled parallel twins) and

▲ IN VIEW OF ITS COMPLEX CRANKCASE ASSEMBLY REQUIREMENTS, SATISFACTORY FULL-SCALE PRODUCTION WOULD HAVE BEEN COMMERCIALLY DUBIOUS.

▶ THE PROTOTYPE 1000CC QUADRANT. IT PRODUCED IMMENSE MIDDLE-OF-THE-LINE POWER, BUT LACKED THE TRIDENT'S AGILITY.

applied it to Page's existing Triumph designs. These included the admirable and thoroughly proven 650 6/1 twin, which had failed commercially because Triumph management had incorrectly briefed Page; the Tiger 70, with its superb top-end engine layout; and the rolling chassis of the Tiger 90. By these typically Turneresque touches of simple brilliance did Triumph escape the usual extended and expensive development period of a brand-new model.

## Bread-and-butter models

It must be remembered that while Triumph had, until the advent of Sangster and Turner, been manufacturers of exceptionally high-quality machinery, it also had experience of tightly budgeted utilities. The first of these was the 225 cc two-stroke Junior, nicknamed "Baby." A strict utility, it grew in size to 250 cc in 1923 and was withdrawn just two years later. Then there was the astoundingly cheap – in every respect – Villiers-powered 98 cc flyweight which sold for £16 16s. But perhaps the machine which best illustrates Triumph's commercial aptitude was the Model P of 1925. At a time when Triumph's own Type SD, with which it may be fairly compared, was on sale for £83, the Depression-stimulated 550 cc Model P was priced at a mere £42 17s 6d. Despite numerous shortcomings, none of them critical, between 1925 and 1927, when production ceased, the company produced and sold about 1,000 Model Ps a week! It kept Triumph going in a period when many of its rivals were sinking fast. What made it viable was not the cheapness of its component parts, but the brilliant new production-line high-volume assembly system Triumph installed for it.

◀ THE LATE AND LEGENDARY BOB CURRIE, A BRITISH JOURNALIST OF UNPARALLELED EXPERIENCE, RIDING A 250CC TR25W TROPHY, A BSA DEVELOPMENT OF THE TIGER CUB. IT WAS AN UNEXCEPTIONAL MOTORCYCLE.

## The Transatlantic link

From the start, Turner saw the United States as a vital Triumph market. During the late 1930s, most Triumphs were imported by individual American dealers against the advance orders of specific customers. One dealer, however, particularly interested Turner. This was Johnson Motors of Los Angeles, run by partners William Johnson and Bill Ceder. Unlike other dealers, they bought in bulk and sold to the retail trade of California. The partners even sponsored their own racers in local events. Turner flew out to meet them, was impressed by their operation, and a contract was drawn up assigning sole southern California distribution rights to Johnson Motors, later to become West Coast distributors JoMo.

Throughout the late 1940s, Johnson Motors' Triumph sales rocketed, and Turner and Johnson became firm friends. Sales of Triumphs during this period were around 1,000 annually, far short of what the Triumph-starved American public actually wanted. By this time Turner had realized that the United States had to be seen as not one market, but two – the West and East Coasts. So in 1950 he set up a wholly Triumph-owned East Coast distribution subsidiary in Baltimore, Maryland, the Triumph Corporation, trading as TriCor. While William Johnson was the man who launched Triumph in the United States, TriCor's president, Denis McCormack, was the man who turned the name Triumph into a major player in the American motorcycling world. By 1951 Harley-Davidson had become so worried about Triumph's progress in both racing and marketing that it complained to the United States Tariff

▼ THE POST-WW2 TRW, A SIDE-VALVE TWIN BASED ON 5T AND TR5 COMPONENTS TO CONFORM TO A MILITARY DICTATE FOR SIMPLICITY. BY CIVILIAN STANDARDS IT WAS SLUGGISH AT 70MPH (113KM/H), BUT THE WORLD'S SOLDIERY LOVED IT. IT WAS THE WORLD'S FIRST MASS-PRODUCTION MODEL WITH AC ELECTRICS.

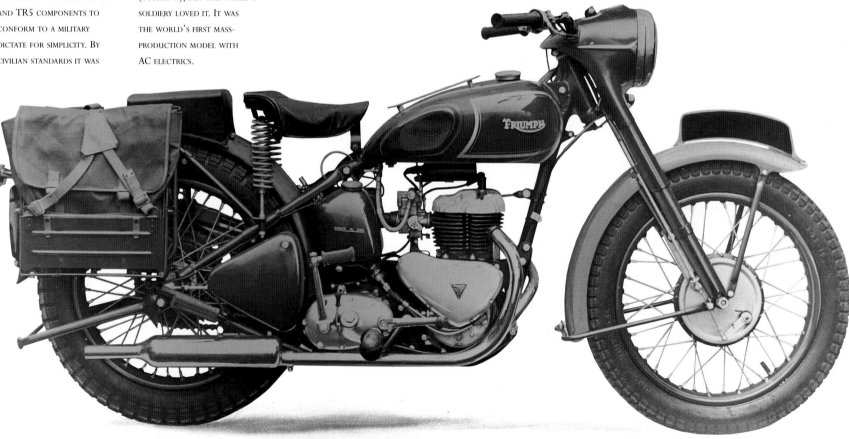

Commission, demanding a high duty on all imported motorcycles. At the end of a nine-day hearing, however, the Commission decided against Harley-Davidson. And now, thanks to all the publicity, Triumph in the United States really got into its stride.

From TriCor came the ambition to beat Harley-Davidson, both at Daytona Beach, Florida, and on flat track. From TriCor came the pressure on the American Motorcycle Association (AMA) to drop its Class C protectionist rule, in which indigenous (side-valve) machinery was advantaged by 250 cc over imported ohv machinery. (In fact, the origin of this rule was entirely honorable – an attempt by American manufacturers to encourage low-cost racing with roadster-based machinery, rather than go the hideously expensive route of European grand-prix exotica). And from TriCor, and Cliff Guild in particular, came a great deal of the racing development that was eventually to bring Triumph victory at Daytona.

## Under BSA's umbrella

Few British enthusiasts even now are aware of the debt of gratitude that they, through Triumph at Meriden, owe to TriCo and JoMo. Equally few American enthusiasts are aware of the terrible burden placed on Meriden middle management (design, development, service, and sales chiefs) by the ruinous fiscal strategies imposed by the BSA Group's pernicious profit-skimming exercises at Triumph. For reasons unclear even now, Jack Sangster sold Triumph to BSA in 1951, reportedly for £2.5 million. It may have been that Triumph lacked the capital to expand both the factory and its American operation, or possibly that Sangster himself had been forewarned of prohibitive death-duty payments; but at that time Triumph was a hugely profitable and expanding manufacturer with assets exceeding the purchase price and with banked capital of something in excess of £1 million.

▲ ARMY TEST RIDERS WITH THE POTENTIALLY GREAT 350CC TWIN 3TW MILITARY MODEL OF 1939. WHEN THE COVENTRY FACTORY WAS BLITZED IN 1940, IT WAS LOST FOR GOOD. IT HAD A TOP SPEED OF OVER 70MPH (113KM/H), DID OVER 80MPG (3.53L/100KM), WEIGHED 240LB (109KG), AND HAD 6IN (154MM) GROUND CLEARANCE.

For a few years all was well, but then business changed. Or at least the motorcycle divisions of BSA and Triumph did. Quite simply, the Group began to lose money. In 1960, when Eric Turner took over as Group chairman from Jack Sangster, who retired, Group profits were almost £3.5 million. A mere decade later, they had become an £8.5 million loss. During this period shareholders demanded their expected dividends, and little was put into motorcycle research and development. To remain afloat the Group began stripping its own most valuable assets – gun manufacturing, small engines, bicycles, machine tools (Jessops), sintered engineering (in which BSA was a pioneer), car manufacturing (Daimler), and others. All were sold, until only the motorcycle companies were left.

Eric Turner, who made no secret of his lack of interest in motorcycles per se, in 1964 brought in Harry Sturgeon to run the motorcycle divisions. Sturgeon, without motorcycle experience, was a capable businessman. In 1967, following Sturgeon's untimely death, Lionel Jofeh took over as managing director. And Jofeh voiced the opinion that his own ignorance of the motorcycling world, far from being an impediment would enable him to bring fresh creativity to a tradition-steeped industry. To prove his point, he opened the notorious experimental center at Umberslade Hall, Warwickshire. This quickly earned the richly deserved sobriquet of "Slumberglade Hall" and gave every appearance of a cross between a black hole and a psychiatric hospital.

## "Tribsa" machines

About the same time, a bunch of industrial consultants was brought in to help, and they recommended that the two great rival names of BSA and Triumph be merged in terms of both manufacture and selling organizations. Dealers in both the United States and Britain went into almost open revolt. This loss of trade faith was compounded by what had become the shocking

UNFORTUNATELY THE TIGER CUB SUFFERED FROM UNRELIABLE AC ELECTRICS AND A PUNY, PLAIN BIG END, WHICH WAS NOT UPGRADED WITH ROLLERS UNTIL 1966.

FAST BECOMING A SMALL COLLECTOR'S PRIZE, A 1957 T20 TIGER CUB. DEVELOPED FROM THE 1953 150CC T15 TERRIER, THIS HANDSOME LITTLE 200CC MODEL OFFERED 60MPH (97KM/H) AND 120MPG (2.35L/100KM) IN REGULAR USE.

unreliability of BSAs especially, but Triumphs also, as triple demons took a relentless grip. The first was the collapse of the factory employees' trust in their increasingly remote management, which led to a spate of union troubles; the second was a drastic lowering of the production, or build, quality of the products; the third was the general dissatisfaction with most of the designs that originated at Umberslade Hall.

In the plethora of new machines that appeared, the most potent symbol of the new madness was the introduction of the "Tribsa" identi-twins. The enthusiasts of both brands hated them because they looked awful, and they had lost their brand individuality; in any case they performed no better and often worse than the models they had replaced.

## The Meriden Co-operative

Eric Turner and Lionel Jofeh resigned in 1971. Lord Shawcross, with the Department of Trade and Industry, eventually managed to sell the husk of what had been two great motorcycle companies to Manganese Bronze Holdings, which by now also owned Norton, Royal Enfield, AJS, Matchless, Francis-Barnet, James-Velocette, and Villiers. The new company, Norton Villiers Triumph (NVT), was to be managed by Dennis Poore, following a £5 million capital injection by both Manganese Bronze and the DTI.

It came to naught. To reduce an horrifically convoluted story to its essentials, Triumph employees, perceiving that they were to lose their jobs when the Meriden factory was sold off by NVT, appealed to the Government, which intimated £12 million support, but which in the end came up with a mere £4 million following the prolonged and profitless two-year union "sit-in" by the Meriden workforce. Eventually it was agreed between the workforce and NVT that the Meriden Co-operative would manufacture Triumph twins for NVT under contract.

From 1975 to 1981, a whole variety of mainly

◀ A T20 TIGER CUB TRIALS MODEL IN ACTION IN THE SCOTTISH SIX DAYS TRIAL IN THE 1970S.

T140-based Bonnevilles left Meriden. In general they were acceptable, but they had lost the old glory entirely, and with the disappearance of the support industries, an increasing percentage of foreign parts was used to equip them. It was not quite the end, though, for when the co-operative finally ran out of funds in 1981, John Bloor purchased all rights of the name and leased manufacturing rights of the twins to Les Harris,

who ran his own Triumph spares and engineering business and had been the buyer of Slippery Sam and was its sponsor in its final three-year racing life. They were good motorcycles, the Harris Triumphs, but Harris lacked the huge financial resources to pay the swingeing American public-liability insurance premiums, and in 1988 the last twin left the Harris plant in Devon.

And there, for the moment, the matter rested.

## TRIUMPH PEOPLE

*W*ithout the spirit of humankind to energize them, machines — motorcycles — are little but an inert mass. To a degree unimaginable to a car driver, a motorcycle relies for its "life" on the empathy of its rider. It is shaped by people to please people. These are some of those who have made Triumphs what they are. To ride one is to communicate directly with these committed folk.

## Schulte

As is so often the case in the founding of a dynasty, its original strength lies in the quality of two quite different yet complementary sources. There is little doubt that Siegfried Betteman was the business dynamo whose drive, ambition, and accounting skills lifted Triumph from teetering pioneer to major producer in the years between 1885 and 1905. Whether he would eventually have installed any sort of manufacturing process connected with his commercial-part bicycle-assembly plant in London is a matter of conjecture. He was certainly astute enough to have become aware of his own technical limitations, because he sought out a partner with strong engineering skills: Mauritz Schulte, also an expatriate German. Schulte, like Valentine (Val) Page after him, was a brilliant engineer whose ambitions were single-mindedly focused on the continual improvement of the products of his own designs. Schulte, however, was also a visionary. Unlike Betteman, he could see where the future lay and managed to persuade his senior partner that if their new company, Triumph, was to survive, it would have to begin manufacturing. Schulte was undeniably one of the greatest of the pioneer designers and development engineers. Long before Triumph began building its own engines, Schulte had researched into the "secrets" of the early internal-combustion engine. His impatience with the familiar hit-and-miss engines of the day led him to design and build what was probably Britain's first wholly reliable and durable motorcycle engine, the 3 HP Model of 1905.

## Page

The Depression of the late 1920s and early 1930s seriously hurt Triumph. The company survived by manufacturing utility models at ultra-low prices. It also ceased serious road-racing contention, and Triumph was in danger of losing its identity. Val

▲ F.B. HALFORD IN THE 1922 SENIOR TT. HE FINISHED 13TH AT AN AVERAGE SPEED OF 49.7 MPH.

▼ ▶ VAL PAGE'S EXCELLENTLY DESIGNED BUT POORLY MARKETED 1934 650CC 6/1 TWIN. MANY OF ITS ENGINE FEATURES WERE INCORPORATED WITH GREAT SUCCESS BY PAGE INTO HIS BSA A7 TWIN OF 1946.

Page was brought in to redefine its motorcycles. Page, who is still regarded as one of Britain's greatest motorcycle designers but whose reserved nature allowed him to become overshadowed by more ebullient characters in the same field, in 1934 provided Triumph with the Mk 5 range of 250, 350, and 500 singles. These were to form the commercial backbone of a product line from which the Speed Twin would emerge and eventually achieve global fame and influence.

## Sangster and Turner

Jack Sangster is seen by many as the most influential man of the entire British motorcycle industry. It was he who bought and resurrected

dying Ariel in 1932 and then took over ailing Triumph in 1936; and it was he who sold Triumph and Ariel to the BSA Group in 1951, with all that that subsequently entailed. He was also Edward Turner's patron. Sangster had a fine head for business and recognized in Turner a rare, almost unique, combination of talents, of which the most valuable was his protegé's ability to achieve profitable commercial success through sound compromise rather than slavish adherence to an ideal. Perhaps for this reason, wherever Sangster went, so did Turner (Ariel in 1932, Triumph in 1936); and whenever Turner appeared, Val Page disappeared (from Ariel in 1932, from Triumph in 1936). Turner also "cleaned up" two of Page's most popular lines of singles, the 350 and 500 Ariel Red Hunter of the early 1930s, and the Mk 5 Triumph of the mid-1930s.

Once Turner had satisfied himself of the 5T's rich potential in 1937, he quickly took over the management of all Triumph departments save that of spares and service. Almost single-handedly he

▲ MARJORIE COTTLE, BRITAIN'S FOREMOST FEMALE COMPETITION RIDER OF THE 1920S, ON HER TRIUMPH. SHE REPRESENTED BRITAIN IN THE ISDT.

▲ JACK SANGSTER, THE MAN WHO SAVED ARIEL FROM THE DEPRESSION OF THE 1920S AND WHO RESURRECTED TRIUMPH WHEN HE BOUGHT THE COMPANY IN 1936 AND INSTALLED EDWARD TURNER.

▼ THE 1947 350CC 3T TWIN. INSPIRED BY THE WW2-BLITZED 3TW BUT INCORPORATING CERTAIN 5T FEATURES, IT WAS UNREDEEMABLY DOCILE AND WAS QUIETLY DROPPED AFTER A FEW YEARS.

designed, styled, developed, and marketed Triumphs, as well as formulating policy and handling day-to-day business. His energy was prodigious, his expectations fearful, his ambitions limitless. Inevitably, he turned to the United States, which he saw in the 1930s was rich for exploitation, its motorcyclists riding mainly admirably tough but hopelessly outdated machinery. He met William ("Bill") Johnson, who was a man of similar business abilities, and both men cultivated each other's friendship with one

eye on genuine companionship and the other firmly on business. Triumph US sales reached such a pitch that by 1950, as we have seen, Turner set up Triumph's own distribution center, TriCor, in Baltimore under the guiding hand of Denis McCormack, whose unshakable resolution turned Triumph, in the perception of most Americans, into an Anglo-American company which just happened to have originated in Britain. By 1954 Triumph had become a major force in American motorcycling.

◀ EDWARD TURNER (CENTER), VALENTINE PAGE (LEFT), AND BERT HOPWOOD (RIGHT). BETWEEN THEM THEY DESIGNED OR IMPROVED MOST ARIELS, BSAS, NORTONS, AND TRIUMPHS FROM THE 1930S ON.

▲ AT DAYTONA, GENE ROMERO AND DOUG HELE IN DEEP DISCUSSION, PROBABLY OVER THE RACING TRIPLES.

## Guild, Hopwood, and Hele

Probably no greater name than Cliff Guild will ever ring in the ears of Triumph racers in the United States. He joined TriCor in 1953 and quickly gained a reputation for preparing T100s and derivatives that were not only faster but more reliable than any others. It is not generally appreciated in Britain that, almost until the end, West Coast (JoMo) and East Coast (TriCor) were operating as two quite separate operations, often in competition with each other. It became traditional that West Coast racers were above all fast, while the East Coast bikes sacrificed a touch of power for superior reliability. Guild's was the wise, guiding hand behind this sporting operation. He contributed almost as much to the racing development of the 5TA Daytona racing models from 1959 as did the great Doug Hele himself.

The names of Bert Hopwood and Doug Hele go hand-in-glove. Hopwood was the elder; he had worked with both Page and Turner, working his way steadily up through the ranks at Ariel, Triumph, Norton and BSA. On the way he designed the Norton Dominator engine in 1947 and redesigned Page's long-stroke BSA A7 of 1947 into a shorter-stroked version that was also stretched into the Thunderbird's implacable rival, the A10 Golden Flash. When Edward Turner retired in 1964 and Hopwood took over the management of Triumph, he immediately hired Hele as his development and race chief. The two men worked brilliantly together. Had they not been frustrated at almost every turn by their board's unfathomable style of management, they would have undoubtedly made Triumph once more into one of the world's great brands. Without question their greatest success was the Trident/Rocket Three which, for all its production shortcomings, was the greatest of that era's big sports-racers.

## Poore

Dennis Poore is often regarded as the final ogre in the sad tale of Meriden's demise. Certainly he was a ruthless businessman, and he occasionally

◀ THE START OF THE "DAYS OF GLORY"? P.H. ALVES, A.J. GAYMER, AND P.F. HAMMOND POSE BRIGHT AS BUTTONS FOR THE 1951 ISDT. THEY WON THE TROPHY.

▲ IF EVER A DYNAMIC INDUSTRIALIST WAS BLIGHTED BY FATE AND CIRCUMSTANCE, IT WAS DENNIS POORE, CHAIRMAN OF NORTON (AMC) WHEN HE TOOK OVER THE BSA GROUP IN 1974.

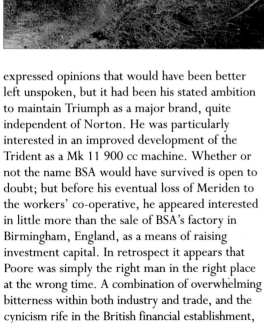

◀ THEY COME NO GREATER THAN KEN HEANES, TRIUMPHANT TO THE CORE — DEALER, COMPETITOR, ENTRANT AND ISDT TEAM MANAGER. HE HAD A GRIN LIKE A SCHOOLBOY BUT THE SKILL OF OLD NICK OVER HOT COALS, AND WAS HARD AND SHREWD WITH IT. A MAN TO HAVE ON YOUR SIDE.

◀ JOHN GILES, BETTER KNOWN FOR HIS SCRAMBLES (MOTO-CROSS) EXPLOITS ON BIG TWIN TRUMPETS, HERE DOWN TO HIS UPPERS IN THE 1956 TRAVERS TRIAL.

expressed opinions that would have been better left unspoken, but it had been his stated ambition to maintain Triumph as a major brand, quite independent of Norton. He was particularly interested in an improved development of the Trident as a Mk 11 900 cc machine. Whether or not the name BSA would have survived is open to doubt; but before his eventual loss of Meriden to the workers' co-operative, he appeared interested in little more than the sale of BSA's factory in Birmingham, England, as a means of raising investment capital. In retrospect it appears that Poore was simply the right man in the right place at the wrong time. A combination of overwhelming bitterness within both industry and trade, and the cynicism rife in the British financial establishment, were probably a guarantee of failure.

## The U.S.A.

By the late 1950s, the British motorcycle press was beginning to report on some of the major American events. For the first time the big desert races and enduros in the United States were interesting British buffs. Names like Bud Ekins, Eddie Mulder, and Bill Baird began impinging themselves on the British consciousness. Equally, as European enduro and ISDT events impressed America, so British off-road riders such as Jim Alves, Roy Peplow, Johny Giles, Sammy Miller, and Ken Heanes won fame in the United States. The model which above all others commanded the respect of both camps was the T100A-based ISDT-cum-enduro model. Here, at last, was truly common ground.

## Tait

One of the great unsung heroes of the development of the racing 5TA is Percy Tait. He worked in various departments at Meriden, eventually becoming chief development rider, as well as maturing into a road racer of formidable skills. To Turner should go the credit for designing the 5TA, to Hopwood for recognizing in Hele the man with the talent to uncover its racing potential, but Tait deserves much wider praise, too. It was his enormous variety of hands-on skills that enabled him to appreciate, then translate into usable performance, so many of the improvements involved in turning roadster into racer.

Because he was, perhaps, too well known as a "simple" Meriden tester, Tait, while hero-worshipped by his British racing fans, was rarely given the acclaim he so richly deserved. By the time BSA/Triumph had decided to take the Daytona plunge with its triples, it was getting late. When Ken Sprayson, the frame wizard, was approached, it was already too late: He could not build the required six frames in under six months. Tait came to the rescue by nominating his own wizard, Rob North, who had already impressed Tait through the chassis performance he had obtained in the Royal Enfield GP5 works machine that Tait was campaigning around that time. North agreed to do the seemingly impossible – to

construct six frames in six weeks. He engaged the help of Bill Fannon and, with no time to build proper jigs apart from some rough-and-ready clamps, the two men bent and welded the frames within the agreed period. Their construction followed that of the R.E. GP5's frame ridden by Tait. Each one was numbered consecutively 1 to 6 as it was made, and each had its tanks, etc., built to fit: it had to be this way because without a jig, each frame varied, although within its given geometry.

Tait was quickly aware that the Daytona "Beezumphs," or "Tribsas" as they were also

known, required steering-geometry improvement, but was unable to persuade the management to sanction the work. It was only when Gary Nixon came to Britain and voiced a similar opinion that this was carried out, the result being the improved 1971 "Lowboy" frames.

On Triumphs, especially, Tait really was a tiger. One of his most memorable races was the 500 cc event in the 1969 Belgian Grand Prix at Spa-Francorchamps. This is the fastest of the continental GP circuits, yet Tait on a 5TA Daytona-based twin achieved an incredible second place, at 118mph (190km/h), behind MV Agusta-mounted Giacomo Agostini, and ahead of all his rivals' specialist Grand Prix machinery.

## North

Until he built the frames of the racing triples, Rob North was a comparatively unknown frame builder, and although success at Daytona won him great acclaim, it brought him no great financial rewards. Twelve frames over two years do not make a man rich! After Daytona he built any number of replicas, most of which were constructed to a higher standard than the originals because time was then on North's side. If the BSA Group board members had displayed the wit to perceive the commercial potential of their Daytona victories and had put sports-roadster replicas on sale, then Rob North might have expected his just rewards. In fact, a cost analysis of such motorcycles was made by BSA Group engineers following Daytona. The replicas would have been cheaper to make than the existing triples.

In the late 1970s, North left England to live and work in the United States.

◀ The quiet Welshman, Malcolm Uphill, winning the 1970 TT. Self-effacing to a fault, he was always the IoM TT enthusiast's great hero.

# RACING AND RECORD-BREAKING

*B*ecause Triumph has not seriously done the road-race grand prix rounds since the late Twenties, it is often assumed in Britain, and more especially by continental Europeans, that Triumph has little interest in racing. Nothing could be further from the truth. The brand probably has more competition success to its name than any other if we include all form of sport — trials, enduro, desert racing, moto-cross, flat-track, TT (US), all the various forms of production-base road racing, drag racing, sprint, and absolute speed attempts. Triumph has so many victories under its belt that an attempt to log them all would result in an encyclopedic volume. Here are a few.

TRIUMPH HAS ALWAYS raced, although not since the ill-fated 1934 team of Jock West, Ernie Thomas, and Tommy Span was forced out of the Isle of Man Senior TT following mechanical troubles on their Mk5/10 "production" racers has the company campaigned in grand-prix road racing. In fact, as Mercedes may be recognized as the manufacturer of the first car specifically designed for racing (in 1901), so Triumph could claim to have built the first "grand-prix" motorcycle. The inaugural I.o.M. TT event, on May 28, 1907, was for two quite distinct classes of bike: twins (won by Rem Fowler on a Peugeot-engined Norton), and singles (won by Charlie Collier on a JAP-engined Matchless). Much less frequently remembered are the second and third placings in the singles race: Jack Marshall and Freddie Hulbert on Triumph-engined Triumphs at race speeds of 37.11mph (59.75km/h) and 35.89mph (57.78km/h) respectively, as compared to Collier's 38.22mph (61.5km/h) and Fowler's 36.22mph (58.3km/h). Triumph claimed that had it not been for Collier's pedaling on hills, Marshall would have won. The officials agreed: thenceforth pedals were banned by race regulations – and the special TT (GP) machine was born. The following year, Marshall returned, and this time he won at a speed of 40.49mph (65.2km/h), beating Collier by almost four minutes, with Capt. Sir Robert Arbuthnot coming in third and Triumphs in fourth, fifth, and tenth placings. For the next few years, Triumph, while not winning, dominated the higher TT placings.

## Brooklands records

Triumph made a great effort with the famous 500 cc single four-valve "Riccy" of 1921. But despite success at Brooklands, the TT races were never to be Triumph's with the Ricardo-based design, perhaps because of their very poor roadholding. Walter Brandish managed second

▲ THIS IS THE WAY IT WAS. IN THE IoM TT SENIOR RACE OF 1912, THE SIXTH IoM TT, JACK HASWELL, ON A TWO-SPEED 3¼ TT SPECIAL, OVERTAKES A RUDGE RIDER, JONES, AT 70MPH (113KM/H) ON THE DESCENT OF BRAY HILL.

▼ A 1925 RICARDO OR "RICCY" RACER, NOW PRESERVED IN THE NATIONAL MOTORCYCLE MUSEUM NEAR BIRMINGHAM, ENGLAND.

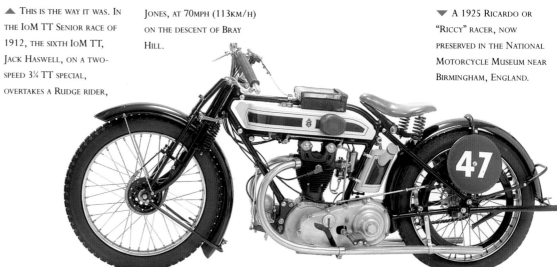

THE TRIUMPH FACTORY IoM TT TEAM OF 1921 OUTSIDE THEIR HOTEL IN DOUGLAS. LEFT TO RIGHT: C. SGONINA, S. GILL, G. SHEMANS (WHO A FEW YEARS LATER ENJOYED SOME SUCCESS ON A "RICCY" RACER), AND H. PATTISON, A PRIVATE ENTRANT PROBABLY ENJOYING PARTIAL FACTORY SUPPORT.

EDWARD TURNER WITH ALEX SCOBIE, LEN BAYLISS, BOB MANNS, ALLAN JEFFERIES, AND JIMMY ALVES IN 1949 AT MONTLHÉRY AUTODRÔME, FRANCE. THE BIKES ARE THE FIRST THREE THUNDERBIRDS PRODUCED, AND ALL THREE HAVE COMPLETED THE 90MPH (145KM/H) FOR 500 MILES (805KM). THE CHAP IN THE BACKGROUND WITH A CRUTCH IS HAROLD TAYLOR, THE AUTO CYCLE UNION'S OFFICIAL OBSERVER.

place at 56.52mph (90.9km/h) in the 1922 Senior TT, but that was all. These models did, however, break the records at Brooklands for the flying mile (1.6km) at 83.91mph (135km/h), for 50 miles (80km) at 77.27mph (124.4km/h), and for the one-hour at 76.74mph (123.6km/h) in the hands of Major Frank Halford.

One of the more audacious successes was achieved by Harry Perrey in 1933 when, riding one of the Val Page 650 cc 6/1 twin outfits at Brooklands, he covered 500 miles (805km) in three minutes under the 500-minute target. The same model, reduced to 500 cc and supercharged at around 7lb. (3.18kg) pressure in 1934, was just nosed out by a New Imperial to win *The Motor Cycle* magazine's cup for the first 500 to better an hour at 100mph (161km/h), although in practice it had been timed at 104mph (167km/h). But four years later, at the same venue, the extraordinary Ivan Wickstead set the all-time 500 cc lap record on his supercharged Speed Twin at 118.02mph (190.01km/h).

## Manx GP success

After World War II came a road-race victory on the I.o.M. that surprised everyone, especially Edward Turner whom, it is rumored, was deceived by Freddie Clark (manager of Triumph's R&D section) over the construction of the first 1946 5T-based Grand Prix model. Clark it was who, with a Tiger 80, in 1939 had established the all-time 350 cc lap record at Brooklands at 105.97mph (170.61km/h). The 310 lb. (140.7kg) bare-bones T100 produced 40bhp, some 10 to 6bhp more than the sports roadster. It was ridden by Irishman Ernie Lyons to Manx Grand Prix victory at 76.73mph (123.54km/h), ahead of Ken Bills (Manx Norton), who had won the event in 1938. While the Grand Prix models were as fragile as most seriously road-raced roadsters, Lyons' victory was no fluke, for in 1948 it was repeated by Don Crossley, while David Westworth

used one of these models regularly and with great success as a member of the Continental "circus" (privateer professional grand-prix contenders) in the later 1940s and 1950s.

By 1950 the Grand Prix model had ceased production, its place taken by optional extras to the T100, turning it into the T100C in Britain and the United States. It had a different role in the U.S., where it was used as a flat-track racer against

Harley-Davidson's 750 KRTT side-valve V-twins. It never seemed fair to British enthusiasts, but in fact HD was heavily penalized by the restricted breathing and combustion of side-valve engines. In any case, while Triumph did not rule the tracks, HD had a hard time keeping up.

Triumph riders were always toward the front, but in 1958 things began to go their way when, in the 500-mile endurance production (roadster) race

at Thruxton (Hampshire), Mike Hailwood and Dan Shorey partnered their twin carb' T110 to victory. The following year in the U.S., the first of the short-stroke 5TA-based racers was making its presence felt at Daytona, first with Everett Brashear's promisingly fast (though non-finishing) rides on the American-prepared (Cliff Guild) 5TA racer. By 1962, the American efforts had proved the worth of the "little" unit-construction 500 when Don Burnett on a 5TA beat not only the H.D. team but the great Matchless G50-mounted Dick Mann.

## Records at Bonneville

On the salt flats at Bonneville, Triumph was ahead of all its rivals. Johnny Allen on his 6T streamliner had beaten off strong challenges from both an NSU factory team and Bob Burns and Russell Wright's Vincent with an ultimate 214.47mph (345.30km/h) in 1956. Three years later, Joe Dudek, an aircraft engineer, designed what is generally regarded as the definitive aerodynamic streamliner, thanks to advice from the North American aircraft company. On the Bonneville Salt Flats in 1962, his project partner, Bill Johnson, recorded a mean 224.57mph (361.56km/h) under the eyes of FIM representative Helmut Bonsch (who was then also head of engineering at BMW motorcycle division). This was followed by the series of record-breaking runs by the Alex Tremulis-designed, Bob Leppan-piloted Gyronaut X-1, which stands even now as the ultimate proof of the old truism that form should follow function, for no more beautiful record breaker, whether four- or two-wheeled, has been seen at Bonneville. Appearance apart, Gyronaut was a fascinating motorcycle which, paradoxically, relied on a Triumph sprung hub to improve high speed handling. Untypically, however, it was employed for its nominal suspension in the front wheel simply because it was spacious enough to accommodate the hub-center steering needed for

high speed stability. The Gyronaut was powered by twin race-tuned TR6 motors employing mainly American power parts on top and British in the bottom end. On pure methanol, each engine developed a tested 70bhp at up to 8000rpm. They were enough to set a record mean of 245.67mph (395.53km/h).

If Bob Leppan had not crashed and seriously injured himself at over 270mph (435km/h) in 1970, powered by twin 820 cc TR6s, and if Denis Manning's twin 750 cc TR6-powered streamliner had not lost part of its shell at around the same speed, who knows what further records Triumph might have claimed.

Perhaps the most impressive speed was that of Jeff Gough's Trident in 1969. Running on gasoline, normally aspirated, and with only a modest race fairing, it was timed at remarkable 169.33mph (272.62km/h). And in 1975 the 1000-cc stretched and turbocharged Trident of Jack Wilson managed an astonishing 192.33mph (309.65km/h)!

## Production machine races

In Britain Triumphs began to take the lead in production machine road racing in the 1960s. When the first IoM Production TT race was staged in 1967, Bonnevilles swept the board, with John Hartle and his incomparably fluid style winning at 97.1mph (156.3km/h). He was followed in 1969 by Welshman Malcolm Uphill, who made history by becoming the first production racer to top the bull's-eye "ton" lap, and a race speed of an incredible 99.99mph (160.98km/h). But the age of the Trident had dawned, and no 650 twin could match a 750 triple in the 750 cc class. Uphill won again in 1970 but this time on a Trident. No individual racing motorcycle has endeared itself to British hearts more than "Slippery Sam." Originally factory prepared, this particular Trident won every one of the five Production TT races it campaigned between 1971 and 1975, eventually hoisting the Production lap record to 102.88mph

▲ THE LEGENDARY "SLIPPERY SAM." NO INDIVIDUAL MOTORCYCLE HAS EVER ACHIEVED SUCH POPULAR ACCLAIM IN BRITAIN. IT WON FIVE IoM PRODUCTION TT RACES IN SUCCESSION BETWEEN 1971 AND 1975, BEING RIDDEN TO VICTORY BY RAY PICKRELL (TWICE), TONY JEFFERIES (SON OF ALLAN), MICK GRANT, AND FINALLY ALEX GEORGE AND DAVE CROXFORD IN THE INCREDIBLE 10-LAPPER OF 1975 – 377.5 MILES (607.5KM). IT WOULD PROBABLY BE WINNING YET HAD THE RULES NOT BEEN CHANGED (AFTER LOBBYING BY MAINLY JAPANESE INTERESTS) TO BAN MOTORCYCLES OVER FIVE YEARS OLD.

(165.64km/h) in the hands of Alex George.

One of Britain's last exponents of racing over closed public highways, George's 377.5-mile (607.8km) race on that three-cylinder old master was of mythic stature and has since deservedly passed into legend. Some mused how could he fail to win on a Trident which by this time knew every inch of that impossible mountain circuit.

When the AMA in the United States finally dropped its rule favoring 750 sv against imported ohv engines, it opened the floodgates, although Harley-Davidsons continued to clean up on the flat tracks, where Tridents were humiliated.

## Glory at Daytona and Mallory Park

At Daytona, however, it seemed that for once the BSA Group had got it right first time. The existing frames were good on the road, but were they good enough? The company contracted frame builder Rob North to cradle the racing engines. In truth it was the BSA Rocket Threes rather than the Tridents which did most of the winning, but the two machines were largely indistinguishable anyway. And while Dick Mann's very special Honda CB750-based racer won in 1970, it was

▲ MARTIN ROBERTS, ONE OF BRITAIN'S TOP SPRINTERS, ON HIS 650 TRIUMPH-POWERED MACHINE AT RECORDS DAY, ELVINGTON, 1965.

▲ ASCOT, USA, 1971. FROM LEFT TO RIGHT: 9, TOM ROCKWOOD; 8, CHUCK PALMGREN; 6, MERT LAWWILL; 5, DON CASTRO; 3, DAVE ALDANA; 2, JIM RICE; 1, GENE ROMERO.

otherwise a 1970-71 walkover for Mike Hailwood, Gene Romero, Don Castro, Percy Tait, Gary Nixon, Paul Smart, and Tom Rockwood. Despite an astonishing turn of speed which left the rest of the field panting, the triples were remarkably standard. They were turning out around 86bhp at only about 6000rpm, which made them easy to ride, and they would rev safely to 9500rpm. It was sufficient for a top speed of around 170mph (274km/h); they weighed around 365 to 375lb. (165 to 170kg). To exemplify the prodigious performance of these road-based racers, in the 1971 Post-TT Race at Mallory Park, Leicestershire, in England, thousands of spectators went wild with excitement as John Cooper, who was then probably Britain's foremost short-circuit ace, beat Giacomo Agostini on his 500 4 MV Agusta grand-prix machine. British enthusiasts had a taste of the old AMA 750 sv-v-500 ohv ruling, and they loved it! Cynics dismissed the win as an aberration – but then a few weeks later, at the Brand's Hatch Race of the South, "Coop" did precisely the same again. And just to prove he was more than a national champion, in the 1972 Ontario Champion Spark Plugs "Classic," Cooper on his BSA played nip-and-tuck with Yamaha-mounted Kell Carruthers and beat him to the flag.

Where did the power and reliability come from?

Mainly a sound design meticulously assembled. The internals were little more than a compression ratio that varied, according to the track and rider, around 12:1; there were either Amal GP or Concentric carburettors of 1³⁄₁₆in. (30mm), gas-flowed heads, special racing cams, followers and rockers, and Quaife five-speed gear clusters. Everyone wanted Rob North Daytona road-going replicas – but BSA Group executives thought they knew better . . .

# End of the road

By the end of 1972, BSA Group engineers recognized the impossibility of developing the

◀ ONE OF THE VERY FEW
FACTORY-ORIGINATED BSA/
TRIUMPH HYBRIDS THAT
ACTUALLY WORKED WELL: THE
BRAND-LESS, LIP-WEARING
1973 ISDT T100 B50 MX.

existing triples sufficiently to compete with the newly arrived and shatteringly powerful Yamaha TZ700 two-strokes. Bert Hopwood had drawn up plans for a completely new range of sohc modular designs based on a new 200 cc single "doubled-up" to an ultimate 1000 cc five. But at the same time it had become obvious that the BSA Group as a whole was teetering on the verge of bankruptcy and plainly lacked the capital needed to capitalize such a major project, let alone a racing team to exploit it. BSA, with its reluctant partner Triumph, withdrew from racing.

Anyone who attended Daytona in 1973 witnessed the final agony of an heroic fight against impossible odds. Dick "Bugsy" Mann, winner of the 1971 (Honda) and 1972 (BSA) 200 Milers, raced an American-entered "works" BSA. Or maybe it was a Triumph: no one seemed sure because it was powered by a "sloper" engine, but was painted Triumph blue. The man of the meeting was the hero of the European grand-prix circuits, Jarno Saarinen, on a Yamaha. As everyone, especially the exuberant race commentators, forecast, he won hands down. No one seemed to notice the veteran Mann's quiet cunning as lap after lap he nursed his off-tune "Tribsa" to within millimeters of its previous track record around the base of the bank. His was an inspired race; yet, in a country in which winning is all, it was, and remains, largely forgotten. Yamahas overwhelmed all, and Mann came home fourth. The reign of the strokers had begun.

◀ GARY NIXON, ONE OF THE
TRULY GREAT AMERICAN ALL-
ROUNDERS, IN PROFILE ON
WHAT APPEARS TO BE A FLAT-
TRACK TRIDENT. NOT EVEN
THE COURAGE AND SKILL OF
NIXON COULD LAY THE
TRIPLE'S POWER DOWN WITH
MUCH SUCCESS ON DIRT.

◀ ANOTHER ALL-TIME
AMERICAN HERO, DICK MANN,
THIS TIME RIDING A BSA
ROCKET THREE IN ONTARIO IN
1972. THE BSA TRIPLES WERE
MORE SUCCESSFUL THAN THE
TRIUMPHS, ALTHOUGH, APART
FROM THE "SLOPER" BEEZA
ENGINE, THE MACHINES WERE
IDENTICAL.

## THE MOTORCYCLES

*These are the focus of our interest. Through them, and them only, did Triumph manifest the skill and talents of its designers and engineers. They were, and will remain for all time, dynamic witness to factory endeavors. Judge them only by the standards of their day; then ponder, which was the greatest of them all?*

# 1905 3 HP MODEL

WHILE THE 1905 3 HP (300 cc) Model was the first true Triumph, and a pioneer to boot, it was for all that a second-generation motorcycle. It incorporated nothing radical, but was simply a sensibly arranged compendium of familiar principles built into an exciting package. The world was forced to follow suit.

Both of the engine's side valves were camshaft-opened at a time when the majority relied on an "automatic," or suction-opened, inlet valve. The crankshaft turned on two heavy ball-races, where others sported mere bushes, and a set of heavy 23lb. (10.4kg) split flywheels within the crankcase ensured the tractability so vital on the gearless, fixed engine transmissions. Moreover, the ignition system, as delicate as most of its low-tension coil type, was, with a modicum of attention, dependable. And, in a period still dominated by uncertainty, the engine was in the right place at the bottom bracket.

## Reliability the key

In fact, even the previous two non-Triumph-engined machines had been successful enough for the expanded factory to have to require a manager, Charles Hathaway. Mauritz Schulte and Hathaway between them produced what must be regarded as, if not the, then at least one of the, very first of the world's truly dependable motorcycles at least equal to and perhaps better than Indian and Rex.

Triumph was also lucky because almost as soon as the 3 HP model was launched, the Bosch-Simms high-tension (HT) magneto was made available to manufacturers. If any single item of equipment transformed motorcycles and cars from the status of playthings of the reckless to useful transportation, it was Robert Bosch's HT mag. With an HT mag-equipped 3 HP Model, a fit and determined rider could genuinely expect to start easily and finish safely any highway ride.

Along with the HT magneto in 1906 came the

introduction of a stronger frame, although one that was still strictly of the bicycle-type diamond layout, and a sprung front fork. Of peculiar design and function, it characterized Triumph for years to come by its fore-and-aft action, rather then the perpendicular rise-and-fall even in 1905 becoming accepted as the best way to absorb bumps.

## Uprating the model

One year later saw the launch of the 3½ HP (500 cc) Model. We tend now to see quick model changes as a modern curse, yet today 10- and even 20-year production runs are unremarkable. In the pioneering days of the motorcycle industry, model mortality was incredible and fecundity even more so. In 1910 came another major advance in the progress of practical motorcycle design, the "Free Engine" as Triumph termed it. The device was actually a clutch of 40 tiny plates encased within a bulky rear hub. Schulte had patented it in 1908

but, cautious to a fault, had refused to adopt it commercially until it had been tested to destruction and to his approval. This little device ranks a close second to the HT magneto in its contribution to motorcycling utility. Until then motorcycles had by necessity been the exclusive preserve of fit young men who alone had the muscle-power and stamina needed to push-start the heavy, fixed-gear machines – or to stop them. Pedal starting on the rear stand now put motorcycling within the scope of almost everyone.

Here was a motorcycle which for the first time was convenient to start easily, then carry its rider for a short trip into, and out of, town. Whatever the actual power development of these engines may have been, an average model would turn in a top speed of about 50mph (80km/h), perhaps more, and, given the right conditions, would cruise at 40/45mph (64/72km/h) – though the shocking roads of the day would have normally limited this to around 30mph (48km/h).

▲ THE FIRST TRIUMPH-POWERED TRIUMPH OF 1904. IT FOLLOWED YEARS OF

DEVELOPMENT BY ITS PAINSTAKING DESIGNER, MAURITZ SCHULTE.

▼ TWIN SADDLEBAGS AND ONE TOOL-BAG IN LEATHER WERE STANDARD. PIONEER RIDERS IN THESE EARLY DAYS WERE BEDEVILLED MAINLY BY TIRE PUNCTURES AND CONCUSSION BURSTS, DRIVE-

BELT STRETCH AND BREAKAGE, SPARK PLUG AND CONTACT-BREAKER POINT FAILURE.

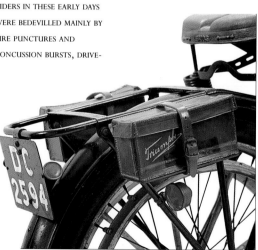

Quaint now, advanced then: two mechanically activated valves, top-grade ball-race main bearings and heavy flywheels (23lb/10.4kg) plus ignition and carburation systems that actually worked. A rare combination indeed.

SPECIFICATION

# 1905 3 HP MODEL

**ENGINE** Air-cooled vertical single. *Capacity* 363 cc. *Bore & stroke* 78 x 76mm. *Compression ratio* 4:1 (approx). *Valves* 2 x mechanical sv. *Lubrication* constant-loss hand pump. *Ignition* LT coil from isolated battery, or HT Bosch magneto. *Crankcase* aluminum, vertically split. *Crankshaft* built-up, split flywheel; two ball-race mains, bronze-bush big-end. *Starting* bicycle-type pedals.

**TRANSMISSION** Fixed engine. *Final drive* V-belt to dummy rim on fixed ratio of 4.50:1.

**FRAME** Heavyweight brazed-lug bicycle diamond-type, open at base; load-bearing engine.

**SUSPENSION** *Front* none (later fore-and-aft Triumph sprung fork). *Rear* none.

**WHEELS** *Front* 22in. (559mm) rim, 2in. (51mm) clincher tire (non-bead-edged); brake: bicycle-type stirrup.

*Rear* 22in. (559mm) rim, 2in. (51mm) tire initial constricting band (later block), on dummy rim.

**EQUIPMENT** Sprung leather seat, tool kit and leather tool bag; soldered and riveted steel tank compartment for 1 gal. (4.5l) gasoline, oil; battery and ignition coil; log book; acetylene lighting.

**CONTROLS** *Handlebar* front & rear brake levers; tank-top carburetor choke; tank-top and mixture levers; ignition advance; cutout (muffler by-pass); exhaust-valve lifter; oil pump.

**DIMENSIONS** *Wheelbase* 49ins. (1245mm). *Weight* 125lb. (56.75kg).

**SPEED** *Cruising* 30–40mph (48–64km/h). *Maximum* 40–50mph (64–80km/h).

**CONSUMPTION** 90mpg (8ll/100km)

**POWER** Nominal rating 3hp at 1500rpm.

**PRICE** (new UK) £43.

# 1911 3½ HP MODEL

THIS WAS THE model that was to lift Triumph from national greatness to global fame. In the words of C.E. "Titch" Allen (founder of the Vintage Motor Cycle Club), ". . . the 1911 Triumph was the first machine of sufficient stamina to permit riders to pass the threshold of physical endurance. The first motorcycle to take more than flesh and blood could stand." In view of Indian's remarkable early achievements, in the United States particularly, an American may disagree, but you get the gist – the first big "Trumpet" lacked nothing. Now, while in geographical terms Britain is a small country, in the topographical sense then it was anything but. Because of a railroad network of unsurpassed sophistication, British roads had hardly improved in half a century. In theory they were asphalt-surfaced – graded stone bound with gravel and embedded in chalk or clay; in practice they became in summer choking ribbons of rock-strewn, corrugated dust, in winter rut-bound quagmires often penetrated by "dragon's teeth" (hidden rocks).

## Endurance records

In this climate, then, did Triumph riders venture out on their personal odysseys. One of the most remarkable was Albert Catt's feat of endurance. On appalling roads he survived 2,557 miles of such physical and mental agony that the experience almost killed him. Then there was the record-breaking Land's-End-to-John-O'Groats ride of Ivan Hart-Davies. This remarkable individual, who specialized in all manner of long-distance record-breaking in cars and airplanes (in one of which he eventually died) covered the 886 miles in 29 hours and 12 minutes. Anyone today who managed an averaged speed of 30mph (48km/h) over what would currently be classified as unmade roads (byways, Jeep trails) would be regarded as a hero. Then, it was a feat of near-superhuman endeavour.

The ordinary Free Engine model had a top speed

of almost 60mph (97km/h) and, although lacking a transmission, it enjoyed the advantage of the useful little rear wheel hub clutch and an adjustable engine pulley. The standard setting of this device gave a gear ratio of approximately 4.5:1, which was enough to deal with most hills and hazards. But by dismounting and adjusting the outer rim of the dished V-belt pulley with a wrench, a rider with foresight could drop the gear to as low as 6.25:1 before approaching a known climb. Such a gear ratio, while high these days, could deal with any known public-road hills.

## Model variants

The 3½ HP Model is generally considered to represent the best of its type and was a logical development of the first Triumph-engined model. It was available in four variations. These were the basic Roadster Model, which came with a fixed

engine at £48, and which everyone knew and trusted. Then there was the new-fangled Free Engine Model as a sort of deluxe grand tourer for £55. For the go-faster brigade, the Tourist Trophy Roadster could be had at a snip for a mere £50, but, like the racer it resembled, it was without a free engine. And top of the line was the awesome Tourist Trophy Racer. This was the real thing – an over-the-counter replica of the factory's IoM racers. It was stripped of lighting, had dropped handlebars, a small and lowered seat, high-tensile steel rims, fully adjustable footrests, and a wheelbase shorter by 2 inches (50mm). With a mildly "tweaked" engine, which usually amounted to carburetor rejetting following muffler elimination, one of these developed enough power to manage a top gear of 3.5:1 and under favorable conditions would get close to 70mph (113km/h).

◀ A TYPICAL HIGHWAY MOTORCYCLIST OF 1910. HE WOULD BE DRESSED IN HEAVY TWEEDS OVER HEAVY WOOL UNDERWEAR. PHYSICAL ACTIVITY AT LOWER SPEEDS DEMANDED GOOD VENTILATION.

▲ THE ENGINE OF THE 1911 3¼ HP MODEL WAS, LIKE ALL TRIUMPHS UP TO THE "RICCY," AN IMPROVED DEVELOPMENT OF THE 1905 ORIGINAL. LATER THE NOMINAL HP RATING NAME WOULD BE DROPPED

# 1911 3½ HP FREE ENGINE MODEL

**ENGINE** Air-cooled vertical single. *Capacity* 499 cc. *Bore & stroke* 85 x 88mm. *Compression ratio* 4.5:1. *Valves* 2 x mechanical sv. *Lubrication* constant-loss hand pump. *Ignition* Bosch HT magneto. *Crankcase* aluminum, vertically split. *Crankshaft* built-up, split flywheel, twin caged ball-race mains, bronze-bush big-end. *Starting* bicycle-type pedals.

**TRANSMISSION** *Final drive* V-belt, dummy rim. *Clutch* foot-pedal-operated in rear-wheel hub. *Gear ratios* 4.5–6.25:1, hand-tool adjustable on crankshaft-belt pulley.

**FRAME** Extra-heavyweight bicycle diamond-type, open at base; load-bearing engine.

**SUSPENSION** *Front* Triumph fore-and-aft sprung fork. *Rear* none.

**WHEELS** *Front* 22in. (559mm) rim, 2.25in. (57mm) clincher tire; stirrup brake. *Rear* dimensions as front; dummy-rim block brake.

**EQUIPMENT** Sprung leather seat, tool kit and twin tool leather

bags; all-steel soldered and riveted tank compartmented for 1.25 gal. (5.8l) gasoline, oil, gas and oil filters; fuel gauge and injector (starting aid); front and rear stands; rear carrier; magneto splash guard; bulb horn.

**LIGHTING** Acetylene.

**CONTROLS** *Handlebar* front brake; twin-lever throttle and mixture control; valve lifter; cutout. Tank oil pump. Foot rear-brake lever. Ignition advance.

**DIMENSIONS** *Wheelbase* 49in. (1245mm). *Weight* 170lb. (77.1kg).

**SPEED** *Cruising* 35–45mph (56–73km/h). *Maximum* 50–55mph (80–88km/h).

**CONSUMPTION** 95–105mpg (3.1–2.7l/100km)

**POWER** Nominal rating 3½HP at 1500rpm.
**PRICE** (new UK) £55.

# 1914 4 HP (550 cc) TYPE H 'TRUSTY'

TWO CONCURRENT EVENTS of 1914 guaranteed Triumph immortality beyond even that of its racing successes. The first was the outbreak of World War I; the second was production of the Type H. Like all Triumphs before it, the H was a development of a preceding model, in this case the short-lived Model C of 1913. It in turn was little more than the last of the old pedal-started range, but with its stroke increased from the standard 3½ HP (499 cc) engine's 88mm to the new 550 cc's 97mm. The C's long-stroke engine developed almost an excess of ultra-low speed torque without any measurable top-end advantage. Charles Hathaway, now Triumph's designer, improved engine breathing by equipping it with improved cams drive gear and bigger valves. The consequences were lusty in the extreme. The H was fully modernized with a Sturmey-Archer three-speed transmission, a multiplate clutch, and a kick-starter. At a time when Triumph's more progressive competitors were turning to chain drive, Triumph limited its chain to the primary drive, the rear wheel still carrying a dummy rim and V-belt.

The civilian market, especially the flourishing side-car market, would have loved the Type H: it was probably the closest thing to a British Harley-Davidson, at least in character, that ever appeared. Frantic for despatch-rider machines, however, the War Office tracked down Charles Hathaway one Sunday morning and, on promise of further orders, he scraped together a skeleton work-force. By Monday morning they had assembled 100 Type Hs. By the end of hostilities on November 18, 1918, the British military had purchased 20,000 of them, and allied forces another 10,000.

## War service

Like no other despatch rider's motorcycle since, the Type H won the respect and affection of all who relied on it. Triumph had for some years used the slogan "Trusty" in both publicity material and

telecommunications. Now, thanks to the utter dependability of the H in the chaos of the Great War, this model became the "Trusty." Legend tells how, amid the mud and blood and tearing steel, the first recognizable form of foot-change was born. Because of the obvious difficulties of hand-changing off-road, "Trusty" riders used a bit of gumption. The standard hand-change lever relied only on one non-positive-stop gear (second). So the riders shortened the lever, bent it downward, and splayed it out a little to enable the rider's right boot heel to lift and depress it through the gears.

Although the "Trusty" was undeniably related to earlier models, it was greatly improved. Its frame no longer bore the appearance of a heavyweight

bicycle, and in all other respects it was distancing itself from its flyweight leg-powered cousin. The main engine improvements were to the big end. A twin row of caged rollers had at last replaced the stalwart old bronze bush (which, once so commonplace, only Royal Enfield would retain until the end). A three-ring cast-iron piston reciprocated with a quietness and reliability that no aluminum counterpart could match even now, and Triumph's own carburetor performed as equably as any modern instrument. Not until 1925 did the "Trusty" disappear from the catalog. In an age when rapid progress changed models in the twinkling of an eye, a production run of 11 years was proof of high quality.

▼ ONE OF TRIUMPH'S TRULY GREAT MACHINES, THE MODEL H "TRUSTY" OF 1914. THIS 600CC LONG-STROKE SIDE-VALVER WAS UTTERLY INDEFATIGABLE, AND MANY A WW1 ARMY RIDER OWED HIS LIFE TO ITS RELIABILITY. IT GAVE TRIUMPH WORLD RENOWN.

◄

A GROUP OF HARD-RIDING ENTHUSIASTS AROUND A TRUSTY, CIRCA EARLY 1920S. THE TOP-GRADE COATS, LEGGINGS AND REVERSED CAPS SUGGEST COMPETITION LEVEL, AND HERE THEY ARE TESTING MILITARY MODELS.

SPECIFICATION

# 1914 4 HP TYPE H 'TRUSTY'

**ENGINE** Air-cooled twin-port vertical single. *Capacity* 550 cc. *Bore & stroke* 85 x 97mm. *Compression ratio* 4.5:1. *Valves* 2 x mechanical sv. *Lubrication* constant-loss hand pump. *Ignition* Bosch HT magneto. *Crankcase* aluminum, vertically split. *Crankshaft* built-up, split flywheel, twin-caged ball-race mains, twin-caged roller big end. Starting kick.

**TRANSMISSION** *Primary drive* enclosed chain. *Final drive* V-belt from transmission pulley to dummy rim. *Clutch* multiplate incorporating shock absorber. *Gear selection* right-hand lever. *Gear ratios* 1st, 13.5:1; 2nd, 8.25:1; 3rd, 5:1. Sturmey-Archer transmission.

**FRAME** Brazed-lug open diamond.

**SUSPENSION** *Front* Triumph fore-and-aft sprung fork. *Rear* none.

**WHEELS** *Front* 22in. (559mm) rim, 2.25in. (57mm) clincher tire; stirrup brake. *Rear* dimensions as front; dummy-rim block brake.

**EQUIPMENT** Sprung leather seat, tool kit and twin leather tool bags; all steel soldered and riveted tank compartment for 1.5 gal. (6.8l) gasoline, 2.5 pt. (1.25l) oil; filters; fuel gauge; injector (starting aid); tire pump; front & rear stands; rear carrier.

**LIGHTING** Acetylene.

**CONTROLS** *Handlebar* throttle & mixture levers; front brake; ignition advance; clutch. Tank oil pump, cutout. Foot-operated rear brake.

**DIMENSIONS** *Wheelbase* 49in. (1245mm). *Weight* 229lb. (104kg).

**SPEED** *Cruising* 45–50mph (73–80km/h). *Maximum* 55–60mph (88–97km/h).

**CONSUMPTION** 90–100mpg (3.1–2.8l/100km)

**POWER** Nominal rating 3½HP at 1500rpm.

**PRICE** (new UK) £63.

# 1922 TYPE R 3½ FAST ROADSTER 'RICCY'

DURING WORLD WAR I, Harry Ricardo (later to be knighted) had been engaged on engine design and development for the British government. Immediately after the war he set up an automotive and engine-research company, with a particular interest in combustion efficiency. One of his team was Major H.B. Halford, who was an enthusiastic motorcycle racer at Brooklands, where he raced a Triumph 3½ TT Racer. It was sufficiently well engineered and fast to impress Ricardo. Independently of Triumph, in 1921 the Ricardo team transformed the engine. They produced a steel cylinder and a water-cooled cylinder head in special high-conductivity bronze. From the old sv engine's cam gear, four pushrods activated four valves around a central spark plug in a pent-roof combustion chamber, and compression was raised from the standard 4.5:1 to a (then) astonishing 8:1. They designed their own aluminum alloy slipper piston (most were iron in those days), and to improve heat dissipation and exchange no head gasket was fitted. The improved engine produced between 24 and 25bhp at 5000rpm. Halford won so many events so easily that Triumph's attention was caught, and the factory engaged Ricardo to develop a replica engine for its own use and production.

## Riccy records

When the first of the racing "Riccys" arrived, they sported almost square bore and stroke of 85 x 88mm so as to facilitate larger valves and combustion efficiency, which was further improved by the adoption of splayed twin exhaust ports. But they were not water-cooled, both barrel and head were of cast iron, and the spark plug was relocated to one side to stop head-cracking. They were power-tested at between 20 and 21bhp.

Despite their reduced power output, the "Riccys" were plenty fast. They took the world flying-mile record at 83.91mph (131.1km/h) in

1921; the following year, with Walter Brandish in the saddle, a "Riccy" took second place in the I.o.M. Senior TT at 58.31mph (93.88km/h) to outpace Sunbeam's 56.52mph (90.99km/h) in the capable hands of Alec Bennett, at the time Britain's finest grand-prix racer. Triumph signed up Bennett for the 1923 I.o.M. Senior. His fastest-ever practice laps promised great things; but he crashed in practice, and that was that.

Significantly, Triumph was forced to accept, by protesting works racers in 1921, that its rickety old fore-and-aft-sprung front fork was no longer up to the job, and the first-year "Riccys," as well as the first racers, came equipped with the infinitely superior Druid front fork. Rudge, then probably Britain's top racing factory, also used Druid forks, so perhaps Bennett had influenced the wise adoption. In 1924, however, Triumph introduced its own normally sprung fork. This was a shame because the new Triumph fork, while tortionally stiff, was so badly sprung that the "Riccy's" handling suffered.

## Cam forms and gas flow

It is believed by many modern Triumph enthusiasts that engine performance of the race-bred Roadster "Riccy" probably has its roots in the puzzlingly pocketed inlet valves of the engine. The feature is more common than many realize, especially where a wide torque band is required in partnership with powerful top end delivery.

One of the most revealing experiments any modern vintage racer/engineer could undertake would be to restore, as far as possible, an existing "Riccy" racer to its originator's specification. A bronze head might not be possible, but a water-cooled iron head fitted with a 12mm central spark plug to reduce cracking might well allow a decent compression ratio to be used. And if the bore and stroke could be squared as well . . . The "Riccy" is one of the curious band of historic motorcycles whose greatness lies largely in its potential.

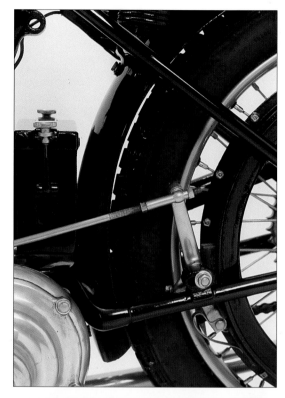

▲ AS WITH LATER TRIUMPHS, THE "RICCY'S" FRAME WAS NOT ROBUST ENOUGH TO DISCIPLINE ITS CAPTIVE ENGINE'S POWER.

▲ THE LAST OF THE EDWARDIANS. THE LOSS OF THE SQUARE TANK'S ELEGANCE IN FAVOR OF THE FAT-CHEEKED SADDLE TANK WAS DEEPLY MOURNED IN THE 1920S.

▼ A 1923 TYPE R ("RICCY")
3¼ HP MODEL RACER –
TRIUMPH'S VERY FIRST OHV 500
SINGLE. ITS POTENTIAL WAS
NEVER FULLY REALIZED.

SPECIFICATION

## 1922 3½ TYPE R 'RICCY' FAST ROADSTER

**ENGINE** Air-cooled twin-port vertical single. *Capacity* 499 cc. *Bore & stroke* 81 x 97mm (racer: 85 x 88mm). *Compression ratio* 5:1. *Valves* 4 x pushrod ohv. *Lubrication* constant-loss hand pump (racer: plunger pump and dry sump). *Ignition* Bosch or Lucas HT magneto. *Crankcase* vertically split. *Crankshaft* built-up, flywheel, twin caged ball-race mains, twin caged roller big-end. *Starting* kick.

**TRANSMISSION** *Primary drive* enclosed chain. *Final drive* ⅝ x ⅜ chain. *Clutch* multiplate, inc. shock absorber. *Gear selection* right-hand lever. *Gear ratios* 1st, 12.46:1; 2nd, 7.47:1; 3rd, 4.5:1 (early racers 2-speed). Triumph transmission.

**FRAME** Brazed-lug open diamond.

**SUSPENSION** *Front* Druid "girder"-type (later Triumph). *Rear* none.

**WHEELS** *Front* 20in. (508mm) rim, 3.00 tire; stirrup brake (later drum). *Rear* dimension as front; dummy rim-block brake.

**EQUIPMENT** Sprung leather saddle, tool kit and twin leather tool bags; all-steel soldered and riveted tank compartmented for 1.5 gal.

(6.8l) gasoline, 2 pt. (1l) oil; filters; fuel gauge; tire pump; rear stand; rear carrier.

**LIGHTING** Acetylene (later magdyno).

**CONTROLS** *Handlebar* throttle lever; front brake; ignition advance. *Tank* oil pump, hand gear-change lever.

**DIMENSIONS** *Wheelbase* 49in. (1245mm). *Weight* 240lb. (109kg)

**SPEED** *Cruising* 50–55mph (80–88km/h). *Maximum* 55–65mph (80–104km/h).

**CONSUMPTION** 90–110mpg (3.1–2.5l/100km)

**POWER** Nominal rating 3⅓HP, estimated 10bhp (racer 20/25bhp).

**PRICE** (new UK) £120.

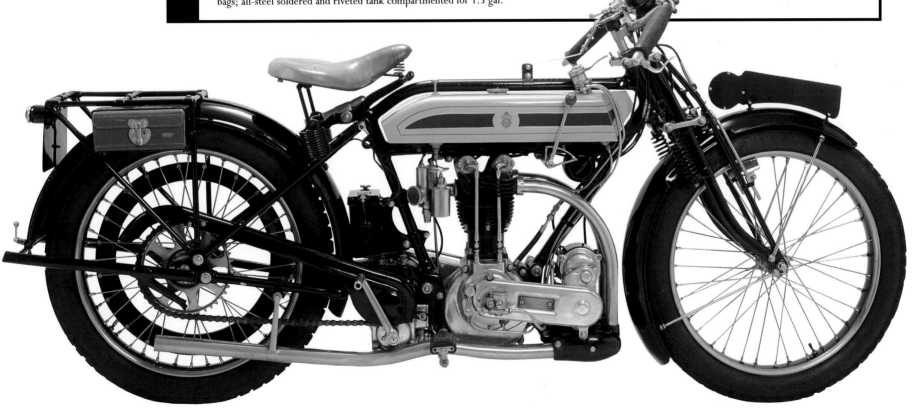

# 1927 TT TWO-VALVE 'HORSMAN'

As THE FACTORY'S commitment to the "Riccy" waned, another of their motorcycles was winning rich rewards at Brooklands. Victor Horsman was less of a road racer in the grand-prix sense than a specialist Brooklands record breaker. At this unique speed-drome, he was one of the rider-tuners who earned a somewhat erratic living preparing other, more affluent, riders' machines for racing, yet preparing them not quite so well that he was unable to beat them to the vitally important winners' purses! During 1925 Horsman was employed in the development of a brand-new big single at Brooklands for Triumph. By the end of 1926 Triumph's Horsman had notched up the hour record at 94.15mph (151.58km/h) to Bennett's 110.58mph (161.93km/h) on the Norton shortly afterward. These were indeed days of glory. Sadly, and despite hopes for the new engine, it was close to the end of Triumph's reign as the supreme British motorcycle manufacturer of both racers and roadsters.

## First of a new breed

Nowadays, most historians identify the Val Page line of Mk5 singles as the first of the new-era models, but technically speaking the Horsman Two-Valve takes priority. In every significant respect, it boasted all the conveniences of a modern motorcycle, and even today could turn in a satisfactorily familiar performance. Its new frame was torsionally stiff (which the "Riccy's" was not); its new forks were robust and well-sprung; its new lubrication system was of the recirculating dry sump type; its lighting fully electric; its braking was by drums front and back; and, oh joy, a speedometer was added. The owner of one of these could expect, like his modern counterpart, to make a journey of all but the most extreme mileage without undue preparation and with every confidence of arrival at the planned time.

Although the Two-Valve was seemingly indestructible, handsome, and superbly engineered, it never quite caught the buying public's imagination. Perhaps the great lure of Brooklands was fading against the IoM TT's greater, more publicly identifiable excitement, where Triumph no longer featured, even though for 1928 a pepped-up "TT" Two-Valve sportster was catalogued.

It's hard to understand the Two-Valve's modest niche in history. The average standard model had a top speed of 75mph (121 km/h) and would, if asked, crack along at a very useful 60mph (97km/h) cruising gait at no more than

▶ VICTOR HORSMAN AND CREW AT BROOKLANDS IN 1926 WITH AN OUTFIT OF HIS OWN DESIGN AND DEVELOPMENT. HIS TWO-VALVE ENGINE FORMED THE BASIS OF TRIUMPH ENGINES UNTIL 1934 AND THE VAL PAGE MODELS.

3000rpm. The TT model was sharper still. A good friend of the author's in the early 1980s owned one of the rare 350 cc TT models (1929–1930 only). Two-up, it had a top speed of 75mph (121km/h), would cruise without stress at 70mph (113km/h) and often cheerfully outstripped an accompanying solo-ridden and finely fettled Sunbeam of the same period.

◀ THE STANDARD TWO-VALVE ROADSTER OF 1928. THESE WERE SUPERBLY RELIABLE SPORTING MACHINES, YET FOR SOME REASON THEY NEVER QUITE ACHIEVED PUBLIC ACCLAIM.

## SPECIFICATION

# 1927 TWO-VALVE 'HORSMAN' 500

**ENGINE** Air-cooled, twin-port vertical single. *Capacity* 497 cc. *Bore & stroke* 80 x 90mm. *Compression ratio* 5.6:1. *Valves* 2 x ohv pushrod. *Lubrication* dry-sump mechanical pump + auxiliary hand-priming pump. *Ignition* Lucas HT magdyno. *Crankcase* vertically split, twin-caged ball-race mains, caged roller big end. *Starting* kick.

**TRANSMISSION** *Primary drive* enclosed chain. *Final drive* chain. *Clutch* multiplate. Transmission. *Gear selection* right-hand lever. *Gear ratios* 1st, 10.19:1; 2nd 6.52:1; 3rd 4.39:1.

**FRAME** Brazed-lug single-loop open cradle.

**SUSPENSION** *Front* Triumph sprung-girder fork with adjustable friction damping. *Rear* none.

**WHEELS** *Front* 20in. (508mm) rim, 3.25in. (82.6mm) tire; 5in. (82mm) 1ls drum brake. *Rear* dimensions as front; 8in. (203mm) 1ls drum brake.

**EQUIPMENT** Sprung leather seat, twin leather tool bags and tool kit; all-welded steel 2.25 gal.; (10.2l) tank compartment for 2 pt. (1l) oil; speedometer; front and rear stands.

**LIGHTING** 6v x 36w Lucas magdyno.

**CONTROLS** *Handlebar* twistgrip throttle, valve lift, choke, ignition advance front brake and clutch levers, horn button, lighting and dip-switch. Hand gear change. Rear brake pedal; left side.

**DIMENSIONS** *Wheelbase* 56in. (1422mm). *Weight* 340lb. (154.4kg)

**SPEED** *Cruising* 50–60mpg (88–97km/h). *Maximum* 70–75mph (113–121km/h).

**CONSUMPTION** 60–65mpg (4.7–4.3l/100km)

**PRICE** (new UK): Basic £66 17s 6d. With acetylene lighting and bulb horn: £69 7s 6d. With magdyno and electric horn: £72 12s 6d.

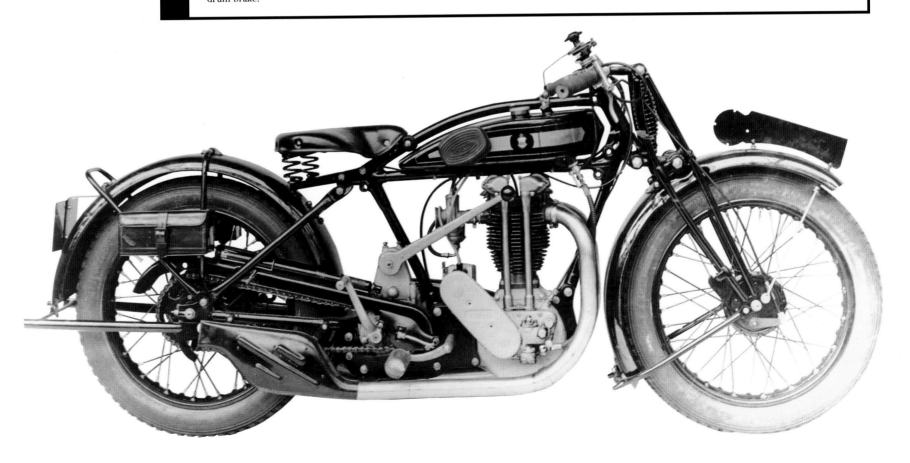

TRIUMPH AT THE beginning of the 1930s appeared to have lost its way. On the heels of the Horsman Two-Valvers came a plethora of undistinguished models, none of which encompassed the Triumph tradition of competition-based development through sound engineering. Fortunately, however, the company wooed Val Page from Ariel, and it is now established that he was the design engineer behind Britain's finest roadsters. His move was eventually to provide Triumph with the principle foundation stone of its post-World War II success.

Page immediately began working toward a brand new line of pushrod singles, known popularly as the Mk 5 line, which first appeared in 1933. They included 250s, 350s, and 500s of entirely orthodox type, yet of the most advanced specification, style and performance. Like no other of his day, Page knew his stuff. His new line was of modular design, in which maximum commercial benefit was gained through the sharing of common components throughout a diverse selection. With the single exception of the 5/2 500cc utility-plus-sidecar special, all now had four-speed foot-change transmissions; and aluminum cylinder heads were soon to be standardized. For the first time a full-loop duplex engine cradle frame held everything together and, thankfully, Page paid serious attention to powerful braking.

## Variations on the 500

In the two years following its introduction, the 500 was offered in four guises. First was the basic hand-change Mk 5/2 at £57. Then came the Mk 5/4, which had the same touring-engine tune, but was fitted with a glamorously chromium-plated headlight and fuel tank, and priced at £65. Top of the roadster list was the sports Mk 5/5 which, at just £66, provided a compression ratio of 7:1, compared to the others' 6:1. This modest lift in fact proved to be so worthwhile that a much

higher compression, 8.25:1, plus various other power boosters, were made available. So well did the 5/5 perform in road racing that it inspired the formidable 5/10, a full-blown racer that was to fill a role played by BSA's Clubman Goldie some two decades later. It was much more than a tweaked 5/5. The frame was stiffened, the engine cradle lowered, and a competition magneto replaced the roadster's magdyno. Unless specified the transmission was without a kick-start crank and employed four special TT-close gears of 7.8, 6.3, 5.4 and 4.5:1. The 5/10 was born in the crucible of Brooklands. It was then probably the best British pushrod big single, but without time for serious development, it remained little more than a short-lived curiosity.

## The Roadster comes of age

Much the same may be said about the roadsters. The 5/5's top speed was a highly creditable 85mph (137km/h), and a cruising speed of 70mph (113km/h) could easily be maintained. On top of that, it braked and cornered superbly. The roadster truly had come of age.

▲ THIS IS A FULL-BLOWN RACER (WITNESS THE RACING NUMBER PLATE); BUT THE ROADSTERS WERE FAST, TOO, WITH A TOP SPEED CLOSE TO 90MPH (145KM/H).

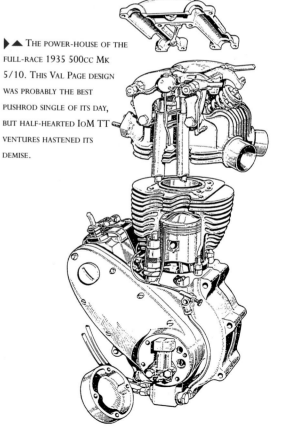

▶▲ THE POWER-HOUSE OF THE FULL-RACE 1935 500CC MK 5/10. THIS VAL PAGE DESIGN WAS PROBABLY THE BEST PUSHROD SINGLE OF ITS DAY, BUT HALF-HEARTED IoM TT VENTURES HASTENED ITS DEMISE.

▼ £70 OR SO WOULD BUY YOU A 100MPH (161KM/H) RACER IN 1934. WITH A CLOSE-RATIO TRANSMISSIION, STEEL FLYWHEELS, FULL-RACE CAMS, AND A COMPRESSION RATIO OF UP TO 8.25:1, PLUS ELEKTRON ALLOY ENGINE CASES, IT OFFERED A FORMIDABLE CHALLENGE TO THE CAMMY NORTONS.

**SPECIFICATION**

# 1933 MK 5/5 [5/10] 500

**ENGINE** Air-cooled twin-port vertical single. *Capacity* 493 cc. *Bore & stroke* 84 x 89mm. *Compression ratio* 7:1 [8.25:1]. *Valves* 2 x ohv, enclosed pushrod. *Lubrication* dry sump, mechanical plunger pump. *Ignition* Lucas magdyno [racer: magneto]. *Crankcase* vertically split, twin ball-race mains drive side, one timing side, twin crowded-roller (racer: twin caged roller) big-end. *Starting* kick (racer: none).

**TRANSMISSION** *Primary drive* enclosed chain. *Final drive* ⅝ x ⅜ chain. *Clutch* multiplate. *Gear selection*: right-side foot lever. *Gear ratios* 1st, 13.3; 2nd, 8.7; 3rd, 6.0; 4th 4.8:1 (racer: 7.8, 6.3, 5.4, 4.5:1).

**FRAME** Brazed-lug single-loop duplex cradle.

**SUSPENSION** *Front* Triumph sprung-girder fork with adjustable friction damping. *Rear* none.

**WHEELS** *Front* 20in. (508mm) rim, 3.25in. (82.55mm) tire; brake, 8in. (203mm) 1ls drum coupled to front brake. *Rear* as front.

**EQUIPMENT** Composite sprung seat, in-frame tool box and tool kit; all-welded pressed-steel 2.75 gal. (12.5l) "saddle" tank, separate 5 pint (2.8l) oil tank; speedometer; front and rear stands (racer: none); tank-top instrument and switch panel inc. ammeter, oil pressure, lighting switch, service lamp (racer: none).

**LIGHTING** 6v x 36w Lucas magdyno (racer: none).

**CONTROLS** *Handlebar* twistgrip throttle, valve lifter, choke (not racer), ignition advance, brake and clutch levers, horn button (not racer), dip-switch (not racer). *Rear brake pedal* left side.

**DIMENSIONS** *Wheelbase* 54in. (1372mm). *Weight* 370lb. (168kg); (racer: 349lb. [158.5kg]).

**SPEED** *Cruising* 70–75mph (113–121km/h). *Maximum* 85mph (137km/h) (racer: 100mph [161km/h +]).

**CONSUMPTION** 80–90mpg (3.5–3.1l/100km); racer: N/A

**POWER** 22–23bhp (racer: 30bhp).

**PRICE** (new UK) £66 (racer: £82).

# 1936 250 TIGER 70

IN 1937, TRIUMPH won the coveted Maudes Trophy by recording some very high speeds at Brooklands with three models selected at random from dealers' showrooms by an ACU official. Freddie Clark on his Tiger 90 managed 84 laps at 82.31mph (132.52km/h); Allan Jefferies on a T80, 89 laps at 74.68mph (120.24km/h); and Ted Thacker on a T70 averaged 66.39mph (106.89km/h).

## Turner's new generation

The Tiger singles were handsomely modernized versions of the existing Mk 5 range. They were the first of Edward Turner's new generation. Val Page had left Triumph for BSA. Wisely, Turner consolidated the multi-model old range choice into three sports roadsters. He completely enclosed their valve gear, gave them all silver-blue-panelled, chromium-plated petrol tanks, silver-blue mudguards, chromium-plated headlamps and a model name, Tiger, that would ring down through the history of motorcycling like no other. The T80, which weighed only a sneeze more than the T70, may well have proved eventually to have been the best of the trio. In its final year of 1939, Brooklands circuit saw Freddie Clark set the all-time 350 cc lap record at 105.97mph (170.61km/h).

Turner is justly credited with designing the 5T Speed Twin, yet what were its origins? The briefest examination reveals that it shares the T70's principle cylinder dimensions, while a little further investigation shows that the combustion chamber, too, was much the same. There of course the similarity ended, for one was a 250 single running a ball-and-roller bottom half while the other was a twin with plain big-ends.

After World War II, the great Alex Bennett had retired from grand-prix racing and was fast becoming one of the world's largest Triumph dealers, ably assisted by his son, Brian (who today

runs his own specialist old Triumph spare-parts business). The two men built themselves a full-race T70 employing a comparatively simple grafted-on top end from a then-current T100. The intention was to take advantage of the T100 aluminum head's superior heat dissipation over the T70's iron. When used in conjunction with an Amal racing carburetor and special cams, the T70's standard power delivery rose from 16bhp at 5800rpm to no less than 21bhp. In such trim did Freddie Clarke's Tiger 70 win the Gold Star award at Brooklands.

▼ FREDDIE CLARK, WHO IN 1946 SECRETLY BUILT THE 5T GRAND PRIX, AT A 1937 STOCK MACHINE TRIAL ON A TIGER 70. THIS COULD WELL HAVE BEEN ONE OF THE MANY HIGH-SPEED ENDURANCE ATTEMPTS MADE BY TRIUMPH AT THE TIME.

◀ A T70 ENGINE. IT WAS PROBABLY BRITAIN'S BEST LIGHTWEIGHT OF THE TIME, THANKS TO A BORE, STROKE, AND COMBUSTION-CHAMBER DESIGN THAT WOULD BE DOUBLED UP FOR THE SPEED TWIN IN 1937.

▼ TRIUMPH WERE SERIOUSLY COMPETING OFF-ROAD LONG BEFORE THE 5T TROPHY APPEARED. THIS IS A COMPETITION MODEL (OR SPORTING TRIAL, AS IT WAS KNOWN THEN) TIGER 70 OF AROUND 1937. NOTE THE HIGH-LEVEL EXHAUST PIPE.

## SPECIFICATION

# 1936 250 TIGER 70

**ENGINE** Air-cooled twin-port vertical single. *Capacity* 249 cc. *Bore & stroke* 63 x 80mm. *Compression ratio* 7.7:1. *Valves* 2 x ohv, enclosed pushrod. *Lubrication* dry sump, plunger pump. *Ignition* Lucas magdyno. *Crankcase* vertically split, twin ball-race mains, twin crowded-roller big-end. *Starting* kick.

**TRANSMISSION** *Primary drive* enclosed chain. *Final drive* chain. *Clutch* multiplate. *Gear selection* right-side foot lever. *Gear ratios* 1st, 18.70; 2nd, 14.00; 3rd, 9.36; 4th, 6.10:1.

**FRAME** Brazed-lug duplex cradle.

**SUSPENSION** *Front* Triumph sprung-girder fork with adjustable friction damping. *Rear* none.

**WHEELS** *Front* 20in. (508mm) rim, 3in. (76mm) tire; brake 7in .1ls (178mm). *Rear* 19in. (483mm) rim, 3.25in. (82.55mm) tire; brake 7in. (178mm) 1ls.

**EQUIPMENT** Composite sprung seat, in-frame tool box and tool kit; all-welded, pressed-steel 3¼ gal. (14.8l) fuel tank, 6 pt. (3.4l) oil tank; speedometer; front and rear stands; tank-top instrument and switch panel including ammeter, oil pressure, lighting switch, service lamp.

**CONTROLS** *Handlebar* twistgrip throttle, valve lifter, horn button, ignition advance, choke, brake and clutch levers, dip switch. *Rear brake pedal* left side.

**DIMENSIONS** *Wheelbase* 52.5in. (1333mm). *Weight* 316lb. (143.5kg).

**SPEED** *Cruising* 55–60mph (89–97km/h). *Maximum* 67–70mph (108–113km/h).

**CONSUMPTION** 90–120mpg (3.13–2.35l/100km).

**POWER** 16bhp at 5800rpm.

**PRICE** (new UK) £54.

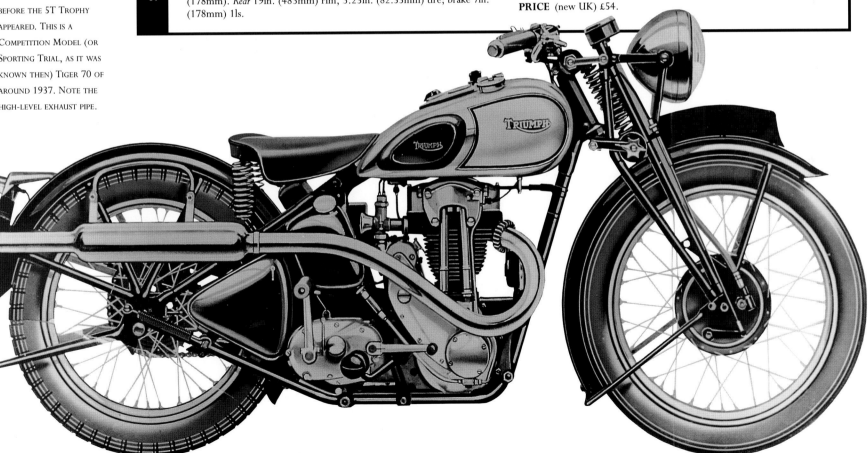

# 1939 TIGER 100

VAL PAGE'S 650 cc 6/1 twin of 1933–36 had not been a commercial success. It deserved better because it exceeded its design brief, which was basically for a heavyweight all-rounder with sidecar suitability and outstanding reliability and durability. It had also earned Triumph high acclaim for its high-speed record-breaking achievements at Brooklands. Its main claim to fame is that it was the stimulus for the 5T and other great parallel-twins.

Edward Turner's genius lay not in origination but in exploitation – in this case of existing designs and production systems – which cost the ailing Triumph company little; and also in the exploitation of the public's desire for the impossible – a cheap "multi" (more cylinders than the ubiquitous single) of seductive sophistication pleasing to the single-accustomed eye. The 5T was acclaimed because Turner had for the first time devised a twin that could be built utilizing existing single-cylinder production systems. The 5T cost a bare £5 more than the T90. Its construction was simple in the extreme: two 360° big-end journals were flange-bolted to a central flywheel, which all spun on two caged-ball races. Two transverse camshafts, fore-and-aft of the crankcase mouths, activated the valves via pushrods.

## The Speed Twin original

The British took to the Speed Twin with the same relish they did to roast beef. Speed Twins remain, in their original specification, some of the most delightful twins ever to have reached production. They were smoother, quieter, more tractable, more economical, and yet faster than they had any right to be. A top speed of around 95mph (153km/h) was attainable, and with the simplest tuning techniques could be much improved. With just 27bhp at 6300rpm, they were top-geared at 5:1, which equated to a theoretical maximum of 97mph (156km/h), and on give-and-take main-

▶ TIMING SIDE VIEW OF A FIRST-YEAR SPEED TWIN. TURNER DESIGNED IT TO APPEAL TO SINGLE-CYLINDER-BESOTTED BRITISH ENTHUSIASTS.

▼ STYLING IS RARELY SO PRETTY. A RIDER'S-EYE VIEW OF AN EARLY SPEED TWIN. THE PACE OF OPEN-ROAD TRAVEL WAS MORE LEISURELY THEN, HENCE THE TANK-TOP INSTRUMENTATION.

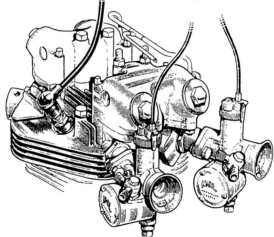

▲ THE FAMOUS "SPLAYED" TWIN-CARB HEAD OF THE 5T TIGER 100. IT WORKED BEST WHEN PARTNERED BY E3134 INLET CAMS AND A RUBBER-MOUNTED REMOTE FLOAT CHAMBER FOR THE (VIBRATING) CARBURETORS.

road cruising, they would nip along at a heady, steady gait of 80 mph (129km/h).

For Americans, however, the Speed Twin was more of an undeveloped racer than a king of the open road. When, one year after the Speed Twin's launch, the Tiger 100 was released, the two

▶ A FINE EXAMPLE OF THE
ONLY "CLASSIC" HYBRID — A
TRITON. THE YEAR IS 1962,
THE PLACE IS BRANDS HATCH,
AND THE RIDER IS DAVE
CHESTER, ONE OF THE
REGULAR "BRANDS
SCRATCHERS" OF THE BEND-
SWINGING 1960S ON HIS HOME-
BUILT T100 ENGINE IN A
NORTON FEATHERBED FRAME.

nations saw it from different perspectives. To the British it was a glamorous rake; to Americans it was a racer-with-lights-on.

## Rocketing US sales

A few Tiger 90s had trickled into the United States, often from British-influenced Canada; but, while it was respectably quick, no mere single was going to convince the average American that it could be anything but utilitarian. The Speed Twin initially, but then the Tiger 100, began changing attitudes. The quick little silver-blue British bikes began to win so many events that the American dealers were selling more than they could lay their eager hands on. The T100's output was 30bhp at 6500rpm, compared to the Speed Twin's 27 at 6300, which gave the sportster a bare 10mph (16km/h) advantage over the tourer. However, for an extra £5 the factory would fit a T100 with a special bronze-alloy cylinder head — and here lay the main advantage. In modern terms it was, at least nominally, "gas-flowed."

10mph (16km/h) may appear to be modest: its effects were anything but, as the replacement of the Speed Twin's pressed-steel front brake drum by a finned cast-iron drum for the T100 demonstrates. With budget-conscious Turner in tight control. Triumph did not provide such items for fun. The T100's oil tank had a capacity of 1 gallon (4.55l), compared to the Speed Twin's 6 pints (3.4l) and a 4 gallon (18.2l) fuel tank was available. The T100's performance was just enough to push Triumph's excellent Webb-type girder forks beyond their adequate performance limits in standard production trim. Their punishingly high unsprung-weight reaction transferred itself to the ex-Mk 5 frame — and the high-speed shenanigans which were to plague Triumph for another 24 years made their appearance.

## Too fast for safety?

In truth these girder-forked T100s were if

| GEAR RATIOS FOR 1937 TO 1949 MODELS | | | | | | | | | | | |
|---|---|---|---|---|---|---|---|---|---|---|---|
| (STANDARD 18T TRANSMISSION SPROCKET) | | | | | | | | | | | |
| | Standard Gears | | | | Wide Ratio Gears | | | | Close Ratio Gears | | |
| Engine Sprocket | Top | 3rd | 2nd | 1st | Top | 3rd | 2nd | 1st | Top | 3rd | 2nd | 1st |
| 17 teeth | 6.46 | 7.75 | 11.35 | 16.40 | 6.46 | 9.36 | 14.83 | 19.82 | 6.46 | 7.08 | 9.32 | 11.20 |
| 18 teeth | 6.10 | 7.33 | 10.50 | 15.50 | 6.10 | 8.84 | 14.00 | 18.70 | 6.10 | 6.68 | 8.78 | 10.58 |
| 19 teeth | 5.80 | 6.95 | 10.00 | 14.70 | 5.80 | 8.40 | 13.30 | 17.80 | 5.80 | 6.35 | 8.35 | 10.08 |
| 20 teeth | 5.50 | 6.60 | 9.50 | 14.00 | 5.50 | 7.96 | 12.62 | 16.88 | 5.50 | 6.025 | 7.92 | 9.54 |
| 21 teeth | 5.24 | 6.28 | 9.03 | 13.30 | 5.24 | 7.60 | 12.02 | 16.08 | 5.24 | 5.74 | 7.55 | 9.08 |
| 22 teeth | 5.00 | 6.00 | 8.65 | 12.70 | 5.00 | 7.25 | 11.48 | 15.34 | 5.00 | 5.48 | 7.20 | 8.67 |
| 23 teeth | 4.78 | 5.75 | 8.26 | 12.10 | 4.78 | 6.93 | 11.00 | 14.70 | 4.78 | 5.24 | 6.88 | 8.26 |
| 24 teeth | 4.57 | 5.49 | 8.03 | 11.60 | 4.57 | 6.63 | 10.49 | 14.03 | 4.57 | 5.01 | 6.58 | 7.93 |
| 25 teeth | 4.40 | 5.28 | 7.73 | 11.08 | 4.40 | 6.38 | 10.12 | 13.51 | 4.40 | 4.82 | 6.34 | 7.63 |
| Transmission Reduction | 1.00 | 1.20 | 1.73 | 2.54 | 1.00 | 1.45 | 2.30 | 3.07 | 1.00 | 1.095 | 1.44 | 1.733 |

anything too fast in standard form for their, or their owner's, good and could in extremis yaw around their steering heads alarmingly. Their straight-line speed did not improve throughout their life, which ended after a 20-year model run. They put on 40 pounds (18kg) of weight, and sadly, they lost some of that old-time smoothness once the stronger one-piece crankshaft had been adopted.

The average British TR5 was supplied with Triumph's wide-ratio gear cluster with origins in the old single-cylinder Tigers of the 1930s, when standard, wide, or close gear clusters were listed (see the accompanying 1937–51 company options sheet). Yet not until 1952 was the United States to get the close gears it needed to make its T100s fully competitive in American circuit racing.

▶ THE SIMPLEST MEANS OF IDENTIFYING A GENUINE PRE-WW2 TRIUMPH 5T MAY BE SEEN IN THIS DETAIL OF A 1939 T100 MAG-DYNO: WHEN PRODUCTION RESUMED IN 1946, THE DYNAMO ALONE WAS FRONT-ENGINE MOUNTED.

THE SPEED TWIN PROVIDED THE FOUNDATIONS, BUT IT WAS THROUGH THE TIGER 100 THAT TRIUMPH REALIZED ITS POTENTIAL — PROBABLY TO ITS SURPRISE, AND OFTEN RELUCTANTLY — AS A MANUFACTURER OF ASTONISHINGLY COMPETITIVE MOTORCYCLES.

## SPECIFICATION

# 1939 500 TIGER 100

**ENGINE** Air-cooled transverse parallel twin. *Capacity* 498cc. *Bore & stroke* 63 x 80mm. *Compression ratio* 8:1. *Valves* 4 x ohv enclosed pushrod. *Carburation* 1 x 1in (25mm) Amal. *Lubrication* dry sump, plunger pump. *Ignition* Lucas magdyno. *Crankcase* vertically split, twin ball-race mains, plain white-metal big-ends. *Crankshaft* built-up, central flywheel. *Starting* kick.

**TRANSMISSION** *Primary drive* chain. *Final drive* chain. *Clutch* multi-plate. *Gear selection* right-side foot lever. *Gear ratios* 1st, 12.7; 2nd, 8.65; 3rd, 6.00; 4th, 5.1:1.

**FRAME** Brazed-lug single-loop duplex engine cradle.

**SUSPENSION** *Front* Triumph sprung-girder fork with adjustable friction damping. *Rear* none.

**WHEELS** *Front* 20in. (508mm) rim, 3in. (76.2mm) tire; brake, 1ls 8in. (203mm) 1ls drum brake. *Rear* as front, but 3.25in. (82.5mm) tire.

**EQUIPMENT** Composite sprung seat; 4 gal. (18l) fuel tank, 1 gal. (4.5l) oil tank; front and rear stands; rear mud guard pad; speedometer; tank-top instrument panel inc. ammeter, lighting switch, oil-pressure gauge, service lamp.

**LIGHTING** 6v x 36w magdyno, 25w headlight.

**CONTROLS** Orthodox British layout.

**DIMENSIONS** *Wheelbase* 55in. (1397mm). *Weight* 361lb. (163.9kg).

**SPEED** *Cruising* 75–80mph (121–129km/h). *Maximum* 95–100mph (153–161km/h).

**CONSUMPTION** 65–80mpg (4.34–3.53l/100km).

**POWER** 30–34bhp at 6500–7000rpm.

**PRICE** (new UK) £87.

# 1948 500 TR5 TROPHY

IN THE LATE 1940s Triumph, like the rest of British industry, was unable to obtain the special metals it needed to properly develop the models attractive to export markets to earn the foreign currency necessary for further development. Then, in 1948 a government award was offered in which successful manufacturers participating in major international events would receive the necessary supplies for further production. It was the sort of stimulus that Turner himself would have promoted in the corridors of power.

## Vale's racers

In 1948 also came Henry Vale, engineering chief of Triumph's competition shop. In order that Triumph might qualify for the Government grant by competing in the ISDT at San Remo in Italy, this genius of resourcefulness produced, mainly from Speed Twin parts, three motorcycles that more than any other were to reclaim for Triumph the sense of purpose it had lost since the demise of the racing "Riccy" in 1926. Not that Vale was actually pioneering, for the Tiger singles of the late 1930s had also been listed in trials specification. Even so, and despite the understandably compromised handling of the pre-Trophy 5Ts, their performance was brilliant. Allan Jefferies, Bert Gaymer, and Jim Alves all covered themselves in Gold Medal glory, and Triumph took the Manufacturer's Trophy – hence the choice of model name.

The secret lay in their engines, which had been originally designed by Triumph to power small RAF generators (bomber battery chargers for airfield use). Being war materiel, they naturally used only the best aluminum barrels and heads, and Triumph had plenty of them. They were light, powerful, torquey, and tractable. Production Trophys appeared shortly afterward in serious competition specification, with increased clearance, short-wheelbase frames, trials seat,

▲ A 1949 5T GRAND PRIX, THE T100-BASED RACING VARIANT DEVELOPED BY FREDDIE CLARK DESPITE THE ANTI-RACING ORDERS OF HIS BOSS, EDWARD TURNER.

▶ BERT GAYMER, A MEMBER OF THE VICTORIOUS TRIUMPH 5T-MOUNTED ISDT TEAM OF 1948. THE OTHER RIDERS WERE ALLAN JEFFERIES AND JIM ALVES. THEY WON THE PREMIER TROPHY AWARD, AND SUBSEQUENT MODELS WERE NAMED AFTER IT.

Grand Prix's were not tne most robust of racing machines, but neither were they as fragile as legend would have it. Had Turner not been so openly hostile to their existence, they would in all probability have matured into the most successful British pushrod racer ever. An example of their performance is to be found in this quite typical race of 1950, the popular Skerries 100. This handicap road race was organized by the Dublin and District MCC around a seven-mile course of local Irish roads. Note that Ernie Lyons was a scratchman with Louis Carter (Manx). Compare the speeds of the four other Grand Prix riders (Lindsay, Roche, Byrne, O'Lawlor) against other riders.

## RESULTS OF THE SKERRIES "100"

| | | Handicap Allowance | Speed mph |
|---|---|---|---|
| 1 | Freddy Dickson (348 BSA) | 13 mins | 69.04 |
| 2 | C. E. Staley (348 BSA) | 16 mins | 66.36 |
| 3 | Bob Matthews (348 Velocette) | 6 mins | 73.83 |
| 4 | Harry Lindsay (498 Triumph) | 7 mins | 72.47 |
| 5 | M. P. Roche (498 Triumph) | 11 mins | 69.01 |
| 6 | Edwin Andrew (499 Norton) | 4 mins | 74.63 |
| 7 | E. Richardson (490 Norton) | 13 mins | 66.76 |
| 8 | Charlie Gray (348 AJS) | 5 mins | 73.03 |
| 9 | M. Fitzgerald (348 BSA) | 16 mins | 64.06 |
| 10 | Louis Carter (499 Norton) | Scratch | 78.86 |
| 11 | Mick Mooney (348 AJS) | 9½ mins | 68.43 |
| 12 | Tom Byrne (498 Triumph) | 7 mins | 70.11 |
| 13 | Ernie Callaghan (499 BSA) | 14 mins | 64.73 |
| 14 | G. O'Lawlor (498 Triumph) | 11 mins | 66.79 |
| 15 | D. H. Campbell (348 BSA) | 16 mins | 63.23 |
| 16 | D. Acheson (348 AJS) | 9 mins | 68.29 |
| 17 | Ernie Lyons (498 Triumph) | Scratch | 76.14 |
| 18 | Wilf Billington (248 Guzzi) | 14 mins | 64.21 |

Twenty-two finished the full distance and two were flagged off with one lap to go.

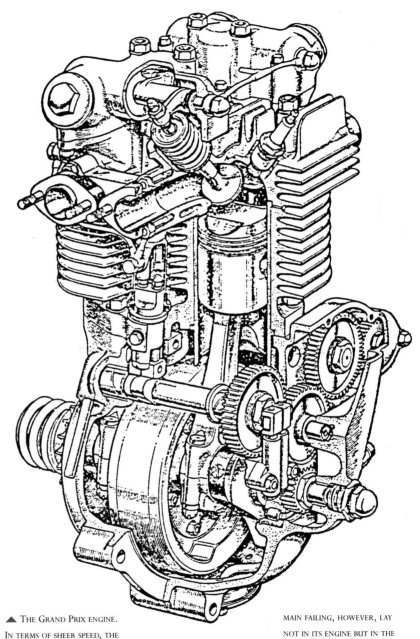

▶ OLD 'UNS NEVER DIE! THE SINGULAR GEORGE GREENLAND (BRITISH SIDECAR ENDURO EX-CHAMPION) RIDING WHAT APPEARS TO BE A CHEYNEY-FRAMED TROPHY IN THE 1973 SCOTTISH SIX DAYS TRIAL.

▲ THE GRAND PRIX ENGINE. IN TERMS OF SHEER SPEED, THE GRAND PRIX WAS PROBABLY FASTER THAN A MANX NORTON, BUT IT LACKED HIGH-SPEED STAMINA. THE MODEL'S MAIN FAILING, HOWEVER, LAY NOT IN ITS ENGINE BUT IN THE APPALLING ROADHOLDING OF ITS FLIMSY FRAME.

small tank, minimal lighting and instrumentation, wide-ratio gears, lightweight mud guards, and the removal of anything not required for forward momentum. At 310lb. (140.75kg) fully fuelled, the TR5 was comparable with a 350 single. Even the most sceptical of modern enthusiasts who rides one is entranced.

## American modifications

Fortunately, it pleased Turner, who enforced a non-racing policy so strictly it bordered on the obsessive. It gave Triumph a powerful American image, which further pleased Turner. And it pleased Americans because, quite apart from its magnificent off-road performance, it was strikingly handsome. In standard trials trim, however, it was not quite fast enough to deal with BSA's and Matchless's big one-lungers, then getting very serious about competition. What followed was to

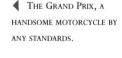

influence Triumph evermore. Americans took the best of the Tiger 100 and even Grand Prix internals, such as 8:1 pistons, larger carburetor and fiercer cams, and turned the TR5 into a formidably fast desert racer. In Britain over the years the Trophy lost its edge in the mud of observed trials which favored the plonking traction of big singles. In the ISDT, however, where speed and stamina are all, it ran for years, claiming victory after victory. In 1954 it lost forever its trials origins and appeared as the no-holds-barred, Tiger 100-powered, pivoted-forked, ISDT/desert racer of great functional beauty.

By 1954 these new TR5s were powerful, churning out 34bhp at 6500rpm (1bhp more than a T100, thanks to a siamesed exhaust system and less restrictive muffler). They were also bulkier at a tad under 370lb (168kg) and had stretched to a near-56 inch (1422mm) wheelbase. Yet still America howled for more!

◀ THE GRAND PRIX, A HANDSOME MOTORCYCLE BY ANY STANDARDS.

# 1949 500 TR5 TROPHY

**SPECIFICATION**

**ENGINE** Air-cooled transverse parallel twin. *Capacity* 498cc. *Bore & stroke* 63 x 80mm. *Compression ratio* 6:1. *Valves* 4 x ohv, enclosed pushrod. *Carburation* Amal 1in. (25mm). *Lubrication* dry sump, plunger pump. *Ignition* Lucas K2F "Wader" magneto. *Crankcase* vertically split, twin ball-race mains, plain white-metal big-end. *Starting* kick.

**TRANSMISSION** *Primary drive* enclosed chain. *Final drive* chain. *Clutch* multiplate. *Gear selection* right-side foot lever. *Gear ratios* 1st, 16.08; 2nd, 12.02; 3rd, 7.60; 4th 5.24:1.

**FRAME** Brazed-lug duplex cradle.

**SUSPENSION** *Front* Triumph tele-fork with rebound hydraulic damping. *Rear* none.

**WHEELS** *Front* 20in. (508mm) rim, 3in. (76mm), Dunlop trials tire; brake 1ls 7in. (178mm) drum. *Rear* 19in. (483mm) rim, 4in. (102mm), Dunlop trials tire; brake 1ls 8in. (203mm) drum.

**EQUIPMENT** Sprung rubber seat; 2.5 gal. (11.4l) steel fuel tank, 6pt. (3.4l) oil tank; speedometer; QD lighting; center stand.

**CONTROLS** Orthodox British layout.

**DIMENSIONS** *Wheelbase* 53in. (1346mm). *Weight* 295lb. (134kg).

**SPEED** *Cruising* N/A. *Maximum* 80–85mph (129–137km/h).

**CONSUMPTION** N/A

**POWER** 25bhp at 6000rpm.

**PRICE** (new UK) £00.

▼ EARLY MODELS, ALSO SHARED WITH THE GRAND PRIX THE EX-RAF GENERATOR ENGINE CYLINDER BARRELS AND HEAD. IN 1951 THESE CLOSER AND ROUND-PINNED BARRELS AND HEADS WERE ADOPTED.

# 1950 650 6T THUNDERBIRD

WHILE THE T100 and TR5 were slaying the opposition, Turner's regular flying visits to Bill Johnson, his United States West Coast distributor, persuaded him of the value of a bigger-engined machine. For Turner, three factors overrode all others: the proposed engine must incur low investment costs, it must conform to Triumph's new parallel-twin policy, and the new model must appear to be a specifically American motorcycle.

When he first conceived the 6T, Turner had not planned for anything more than a 28bhp, 7000rpm sports-touring engine. He was all too aware of the inherent weaknesses of the 360° parallel twin, which are mainly those of the damaging effects of high-rpm-induced vibration resulting from the practically unavoidable heavy out-of-balance masses. His choice of the name Thunderbird (a mythological Native American bird-god) was inspired, as was his insistence on the 6T's American inspiration. In fact, it was nothing more nor less than a Speed Twin replica with bigger holes in the engine.

## American welcome

When the first 6Ts arrived in the United States, they were welcomed more for their potential than for their reality: they were a drab blue-gray in appearance, and their performance, while torquey and smooth, was no better than a T100's. From Turner's point of view this is understandable. The crankshaft of the 5T consisted of two overhung big-end journals flange-bolted to a central cast-iron flywheel. At

that time the factory did not have the technology to forge such a complicated crankshaft, so there was no commercially expedient alternative.

Turner made much of Triumph's American orientation. Despite this the 6T still went to the United States with a mere 7:1 compression ratio, which was close to the maximum possible on the 72-octane fuel available in post-World War II Britain. (Americans enjoyed 87 octane, which was known to support a 8.5:1 compression ratio.) The first batch of 6Ts left the factory with an ex-T100-size carburettor of 1in. (25mm) throat size. American dealers protested, and as a consequence 1¹⁄₁₆in. (26.5mm) carburetors were added which, despite the modest size increase, gave the 6T enough extra top-end power to please most folks. These later models also enjoyed a brighter metallic blue and some chrome trim.

## Long-distance testing at Montlhéry

That the Thunderbird was swift was never in question. Under ACU supervision in 1949, the three first production models, in the hands of Alex Scobie, Bob Manns and Jimmy Alves, went to Montlhéry Autodrôme, south of Paris, with the intention of recording 500 miles (805km) at 90mph (145km/h). In running time they achieved this, but including stops, their speeds were 90.30 (145.4), 90.93 (146.4), and 86mph (138.5km/h) respectively. The lower speed of the last was a portent for the future: it was caused by stops following a split fuel tank (replaced) and a cracked

▼ THE FINAL FORM OF THE THUNDERBIRD. IT WAS COMMENDABLY DOCILE AND RELIABLE, YET FOR ALL ITS TECHNICAL PROGRESS (37BHP COMPARED TO ITS ORIGINAL 30), IT LACKED ITS FOREBEAR'S GREAT CHARM.

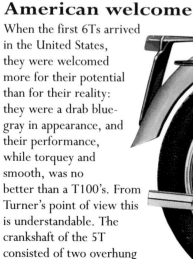

▼ BY GENERAL CONSENSUS AMONG THOSE OF EXPERIENCE, THE SU-CARBURATED THUNDERBIRD OF THE MID-1950S WAS THE SWEETEST-NATURED TWIN TRIUMPH EVER PRODUCED.

SPECIFICATION

# 1952 650 6T THUNDERBIRD

**ENGINE** Air-cooled parallel twin. *Capacity* 649cc. *Bore & stroke* 71 x 82mm. *Compression ratio* 7:1. *Valves* 4 x ohv pushrod. *Carburation* 1 x ⅛₆in. (26.5mm) c/v SU. *Lubrication* dry sump, plunger pump. *Ignition* Lucas K2F magneto. *Crankcase* vertically split, twin ball-race mains, plain split-shell big-ends, crankshaft built-up, central flywheel. *Starting* kick.

**TRANSMISSION** *Primary drive* chain. *Final drive* chain. *Clutch* multi-plate. *Gear selection* right-side foot lever. *Gear ratios* 1st, 11.20; 2nd, 7.75; 3rd, 5.45; 4th, 4.57:1.

**FRAME** Brazed-lug single-loop duplex engine cradle.

**SUSPENSION** *Front* Triumph tele-fork with rebound hydraulic damping. *Rear* Triumph Sprung Hub.

**WHEELS** *Front* 19in. (482.5mm) rim, 3.25in. (82.5mm) tire; 1ls 8in. (203mm) drum brake. *Rear* as front, but with 3.5in. (89mm) tire.

**EQUIPMENT** Composite sprung or dual seat, tool box with tool kit; 4 gal. (18l) fuel tank, 6pt. (3.4l) oil tank; headlight "nacelle" inc. speedometer, ammeter, lighting switch and speedometer; front and rear stands.

**LIGHTING** 6v x 50w dynamo, 36w headlight.

**CONTROLS** Orthodox British layout.

**DIMENSIONS** *Wheelbase* 55in. (1397mm). *Weight* 370lb. (168kg).

**SPEED** *Cruising* 80mph (129km/h). *Maximum* 93–97mph (150–156km/h).

**CONSUMPTION** 65–80mpg (4.3–3.43l/100km).

**POWER** 30–34bhp at 6500–7000rpm.

**PRICE** (new UK) £244.

rear chain guard (removed). Even then the destructive devil of vibration had begun to take its toll. British enthusiasts, familiar with road racing, were hugely impressed with the Thunderbird's stamina. Americans barely noticed, however, showing much greater interest in Walt Fulton's Thunderbird racer victory in the 1951 Catalina Grand Prix and the Johnson Motors-prepared, Bobby Turner-ridden Thunderbird's record-breaking 132.26mph (212.94km/h) at Bonneville the same year. The extra power came from twin carbs, high-compression American pistons, and Grand Prix cams. After two years, the Thunderbird was equipped with an SU carburetor. It improved an already superb tourer into one of sheer excellence. Compared with the Amal's mechanically induced four steps of carburation (idle jet, cutaway, needle, and main jet), which should be but are not always progressive, the constant velocity SU was a marvel.

## Technical blunder

If ever Triumph blundered technically, it was by its employment of the notorious Sprung Hub. Apart from dawdling tourists, few people liked it, and most competitors discarded it. In 1954 the model was radically improved with an alternator, swinging-fork rear suspension, a heftier one-piece crankshaft, and bigger bearings; and in 1956 the lovely SU carburettor was replaced by one of the new Amal Monobloc instruments. Paradoxically these advanced features largely destroyed the sweet magic of the old Thunderbird. It was noticeably coarser, somewhat vibratory, less tractable, heavier, less reliable (especially the appalling Lucas electrics), thirstier, yet no faster. Such is progress! It struggled on until 1962 and died unlamented.

▶ AMERICAN TOURISTS IN BRITAIN IN THE EARLY 1950S ON THEIR THUNDERBIRDS. TRIUMPH OFTEN SOLD MODELS IN BRITAIN TO OVERSEAS VISITORS, WHO THEN SHIPPED THEM HOME AFTER THE HOLIDAY.

# 1955 650 TR6 TROPHY

THE SPRUNG HUB TR5 may not have handled at all well, even off-road, but it did weigh only 340lb. (154kg). But when it put on another 40lb. (18kg) in 1954 with the advent of a heavier frame with pivoted-fork rear suspension, it was too much. And while it was still competitive against BSA Goldies and Matchless G80s, these rapidly improving 500 singles were challenging Triumph supremacy. American desert racers, as always, cheerfully insisted with awesome confidence that they wanted bigger and better Triumphs. They got them in the form of the TR6, a motorcycle which should be regarded as the first true American Trumpet, if only because – with the single exception of the annual ISDT – no major British or European event catered for big off-road racers. Meriden listened carefully to the new Triumph Corporation, the company-owned East Coast distributors, and built a 650 to suit AMA desert-racing regulations.

## Power gain

Because so much was interchangeable, the task was comparatively simple, consisting mainly of installing one of the two-year-old T110 sports 650s into an existing TR5 rolling chassis. Ex-factory, it weighed 365lb. (166kg), barely 5lb. (2.3kg) more than the TR5 desert racer – yet its engine developed 42bhp compared to the TR5's 32. It amounted to a 21 percent power-to-weight ratio improvement and a mighty torque boost low down. Once more, BSA and Matchless riders were seriously disadvantaged.

The only mystery is why Meriden did not use the hefty bash plate, more suitable handlebars and tires, competition rear-suspension units, and uprated exhaust system – all of which were added by American buyers. The engine was amply powerful and reliable, requiring little more than the usual personal refettling and minor tune-up. With suitable gearing one of these formidable

"Desert Sleds" would burst through to 105mph (169km/h) without fuss. The T110 engine was much more than a boosted 6T, of course. To cope with the extra power, Triumph engineers had beefed up the whole bottom end with larger main bearings and a hefty one-piece crankshaft with bigger big-end journals. Top-end improvements were a larger carburetor, a compression lift to 8.5:1, and a much improved aluminum cylinder head with better porting and bigger valves; and, at the heart of it all, new sports cams.

In the U.S. the TR6 was top of its pile by miles, winning the great desert races and enduros so regularly they became Triumph charity races: the Greenhorn Enduro, the Big Bear Run, the Jack Pine, and others were swamped by Triumph riders and winners.

## Handling problems

The TR6 was good, very good indeed; but while American desert racers seemed unconcerned about its questionable handling, the problem in Britain, where road racing ruled, was critical. The root of the trouble was in the swinging-fork pivot. It was located in the center of what, in the old days, would have been referred to as the "saddle tube," and when subject to the ultra-high lateral stresses of road-race cornering, it twisted this perpendicular tube into a replication of a torsion bar.

It was cured to everyone's satisfaction in 1962 when Bert Hopwood, BSA/Triumph Group head of engineering and design, brought in Doug Hele from Norton as development engineer. The 650 engines joined the 500s as unit construction, and Hele completely redesigned the frames. The 1960/62 duplex frame had been rejected by both Britain and America for its down-tube fractures, caused possibly by harmonic resonance (by this time severe vibration-induced unreliability was beginning to seriously affect the 650s). Its place was taken by a new frame whose salient feature

was the robust anchorage of the swinging fork on heavy steel plates bolted to the transmission as well as to the frame itself. There were minor changes in steering geometry and – a hint of what lay ahead – the replacement of Triumph's tele-forks by BSA's own, which, admittedly, were better.

In 1963 the United States got the model it had always wanted: the legendary TR6SC. The TR6 had been an East Coast racer; the TR6SC was pure Mojave. By this time the Bonneville had been born, and the TR6SC, with its new rolling chassis, was powered by what amounted to a single-carburetor T120 Bonneville which, with a free-breathing exhaust system, was equaling the Bonneville's 46bhp at 6500rpm. It was very, very fast, on- or off-road, and it gave Triumph the wherewithal to dominate the deserts and enduros right through to the 1970s.

◄ ROY PEPLOW WAS FAMOUS FOR HIS PEERLESS TRIALS EXPLOITATION OF THE TIGER CUB, BUT HERE HE IS DEMONSTRATING AN EQUAL CAPABILITY WITH A 650 TR6 TROPHY IN THE 1965 ISDT.

▼ NEVER FULLY APPRECIATED IN BRITAIN, THE TR6 WAS THE FIRST TRULY AMERICAN TRIUMPH, AND FROM 1955 ON IT SWEPT ALL BEFORE IT IN ITS RACING CLASSES STATESIDE. LATER, IT WAS NOT SO MUCH BEATEN AS OVERTAKEN BY CIRCUMSTANCES BEYOND ITS CONTROL.

## SPECIFICATION

# 1955 650 TR6 TROPHY

**ENGINE** Air-cooled parallel twin. *Capacity* 649cc. *Bore & stroke* 71 x 82mm. *Compression ratio* 8.5:1. *Valves* 4 x ohv pushrod. *Carburation* 1¹⁄₁₆in. (27.5mm) Amal Monobloc. *Lubrication* dry sump, plunger pump. *Ignition* Lucas "Wader" K2F magneto. *Crankcase* vertically split, twin ball-race mains, plain shell big-ends. Crankshaft one-piece forging with radially bolted central flywheel. *Starting* kick.

**TRANSMISSION** *Primary drive* chain. *Final drive* chain. *Clutch* multi-plate. *Gear selection* right-side foot lever. *Gear ratios* 1st, 13.2; 2nd, 9.13; 3rd, 6.42; 4th, 5.40:1 (close ratios to order with 9.45:1 gear).

**FRAME** Brazed-lug single-loop duplex engine cradle.

**SUSPENSION** *Front* Triumph tele-fork with rebound hydraulic dumping. *Rear* swinging fork on Girling units.

**WHEELS** *Front* 19in. (483mm) rim, 4in. (102mm) enduro tire; *brake* 8in. (203mm) 1ls drum. *Rear* as front, *brake* 7in. (179mm).

**EQUIPMENT** Dual seat; bash plate; competition exhaust; 3 gal. (13.6l) steel fuel tank; reinforced mud guard; no lighting or instrumentation.

**CONTROLS** Orthodox British layout.

**DIMENSIONS** *Wheelbase* 55.5in. (1410mm). *Weight* 365lb. (165.7kg).

**SPEED** 105mph (169km/h) +

**CONSUMPTION** N/A.

**POWER** 42bhp at 6500rpm.

**PRICE** (new UK) £256.

# 1963 650 T120 BONNEVILLE

PARADOXICALLY, THE BONNEVILLE never quite achieved the same legendary status among American enthusiasts as it did with the British. Yet not only was its name borrowed from the famous salt flats in Utah: the development of its engine owed a great deal to American racers. It was their insistent demands for ever more power for their beloved TR6 Trophy which brought about the legendary "splayed" twin-carb head for the T110, the T120's forebear. And it was on this American TR6 that the equally legendary E3134 camshaft first made its appearance as a stock production item. These TR6s were much faster than an ordinary T110 and were, to all intents, dirt Bonnevilles.

When it first appeared in 1959, the Bonneville was actually little more than a twin-carb Tiger One Ten, but wearing as standard the optional extra T110 twin carburettors and the E3134 inlet camshaft. Curiously, with the Bonneville's introduction, when there was a need to put the emphasis on power and speed, the company's earlier 42bhp claim for the T110 mysteriously fell to 40bhp.

The choice of name? Triumph, especially in the United States, was smarting from the FIM's refusal to recognize Johnny Allen's 1956 World Speed Record bid of 214.4mph (345.2km/h) in his Triumph-engined (two 6Ts in tandem) streamliner on the Bonneville salt flats (the AMA accepted the record). Then two years later Bill Johnson on a race-tuned T110 broke the American Class C record at an astonishing 147.32mph (237.18km/h) in 1968. The name Bonneville for Meriden's new flagship was a triumphant yell, with a mild raspberry thrown in.

## Tuning for performance

A power claim of 46bhp at 6500rpm suggested that the T120 model number could be matched in miles per hour. In practice the average road-going

Bonnie would manage something between 112 and 117mph (180–188km/h) in good conditions. But with the help of a range of advice and components from the factory, a T120 could be turned into a genuine 55bhp+ 130mph (219km/h)+ racer. In 1968, for instance, Rod Gould riding a factory T120R Thruxton in the IoM production TT race was timed at 140mph (225km/h) past the Highlander pub – and that was not its absolute maximum! But, like most of the Triumph twins (and triples), they responded better, and more reliably, to expert blueprinting than to power-part installation.

## The Bonneville

The Hele Bonneville of 1963 was a brand-new motorcycle. With Bert Hopwood behind him, Hele designed a new frame, which at last put Triumph on an equal footing with its rivals BSA and Norton. He also unified engine and transmission. The twin improvements were part of an interrelated and corporate whole. The entire power unit was shortened and stiffened, and with the loss of the separate transmission, it was utilized as a load-bearing member. By means of compact steel plates, a 650 Triumph's swinging-fork pivot was securely anchored at each end for the first time, thus successfully resisting the fast-cornering-induced lateral forces that had previously warped the rear end. Up front the steering head was strengthened and improved steering geometry adopted, although this took a couple more years to finally settle at a 62° steering-head angle.

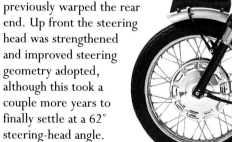

◀ IN 1963 DOUG HELE, FRESH FROM NORTON, AT LAST (TOO LATE PERHAPS) GAVE TRIUMPH FRAMES THE TORSIONAL STIFFNESS THEY HAD BEEN LACKING FROM TIME IMMEMORIAL. HE BRACED THE SWINGING-ARM ROOT AND THE STEERING HEAD.

▶ 650 TRUMPETS WERE NOTHING IF NOT ADAPTABLE. HERE ARE GRASS-TRACK CHARIOTEERS RON YOUNG AND BOB PENN AT SITTINGBOURNE, KENT, ENGLAND, 1963.

◀ THE FINAL DEVELOPMENT — PERHAPS EVEN THE ULTIMATE DEVELOPMENT — OF THE CLASSIC BRITISH PARALLEL TWIN: THE BONNEVILLE. NOT ALWAYS A GOOD BIKE, OFTEN A BAD ONE — BUT UNDENIABLY A GREAT AND MUCH-LOVED MACHINE OF HISTORIC IMPORT.

By this time, Triumph race engineers had overcome a third serious shortcoming – the Lucas coil-ignition system. The damage this deplorably designed and manufactured piece of kit inflicted on the T120's reputation cannot be exaggerated. BSA's twins and singles appeared to suffer even more than Triumph models, but the scrap value of the mountain of holed pistons discarded by Triumph mechanics could have recapitalized the despairing BSA Group. The pre-unit Bonneville had been wisely allowed to retain its magneto, but the unit model was coil-equipped.

## Customized timing systems

Racers overcame this by employing the now-famous remote, quill-driven system, but the ordinary rider often struggled on innocently wondering why his beloved Bonnie did not match up to its popular image. Nor was the equally reprehensible AC charging system any better. A decade old, it persisted in stripping the paint off roadster T120s (and others) by boiling the battery through over-charging.

Those in the know reground the contact-breaker cam to provide a "slow" ramp behind the previously stepped cam. It eliminated contact-point bounce and reliability was assured, even if timing accuracy was still impossible. Timing problems persisted until 1968 when Lucas belatedly accepted responsibility for its ignition system and began manufacturing a contact-breaker set with individually adjustable points. For a further three years only, the Bonneville survived in what should have been peak form, but it was almost too late.

## Two favourite 'Bonnies'

Two model variants achieved almost mythic status in their own brief lifetime. Americans would kill for the TT racer (flat track but with a jump or two): the T120C TT was *the* big Trumpet. It was

reputed to develop almost 55bhp at 6500rpm, thanks to a 12:1 compression ratio, twin 1 3/16in. Monoblocs, open exhaust pipes that ended where mufflers usually began, and enough aluminum components to drop its weight to little more than 350lb. (159kg). The top speed of this basically dirt racer was over 120mph (193km/h). They were produced in small batches between 1963 and 1966 for the U.S. only. The British were equally in love

with the T120R Thruxton. It was equally rare but was a road racer, primarily a long-distance road racer, manufactured at the same period. It was named after the 1st, 2nd, and 3rd Bonneville placings in the 1969 500 Mile Thruxton endurance race. The teams respectively were Percy Tait/Malcolm Uphill, John Cooper/Steve Jolly, and Len Phelps/Chris Carr. Triumphs also came home in 5th, 6th, and 7th places.

▲ TRIUMPH TANK BADGES CHANGED THROUGH THE YEARS, BUT THE LOGO REMAINED AS SECURE AS THE ROCK OF GIBRALTAR.

▼ 1968 T120 BONNEVILLE, CONSIDERED NOW BY THE GOURMETS IN MERIDEN'S KITCHEN TO BE ABOUT THE BEST OF ITS GENRE. IT HANDLED WELL AND HAD RELIABLE ELECTRICS, AND WAS LET DOWN ONLY BY POOR PRODUCTION QUALITY, EASILY REMEDIED NOW.

**SPECIFICATION**

# 1963 650 T120 BONNEVILLE

**ENGINE** Air-cooled parallel twin, in-unit with transmission. *Capacity* 649cc. *Bore & stroke* 71 x 82mm. *Compression ratio* 8.5:1. *Valves* 4 x ohv pushrod. *Carburation* 2 x 1³⁄₁₆in. (30mm) Amal Monoblocs. *Lubrication* dry sump, plunger pump. *Ignition* Lucas 12v coil. *Crankcase* vertically split, twin ball-race mains, plain shell big-ends, crankshaft one-piece forging with radially-bolted central flywheel. *Starting* kick. *Generator* crankshaft A.C.

**TRANSMISSION** *Primary drive* triplex chain. *Transmission* shock-absorber rubbers in rear wheel. *Gear selection* right-side foot lever. *Gear ratios* 1st, 11.81; 2nd, 8.17; 3rd, 5.76; 4th, 4.84:1 (close ratios to order).

**FRAME** Brazed-lug single-loop duplex engine cradle.

**SUSPENSION** *Front* ex-BSA tele-fork with two-way damping. *Rear* swinging fork on Girling units.

**WHEELS** *Front* 3.25in. (83mm) tire, 18in. (457mm) rim. *Brake* 8in. (203mm) 1ls drum. *Rear* 3.5in. (89mm) tire. 18in. (457mm) rim. *Brake* 7in. (178mm) 1ls drum.

**EQUIPMENT** Dual seat; 4 gal. (18l) steel fuel tank; tool kit; tank-top luggage grid; rev-counter; 6pt. (3.4l) oil tank; grab rail, hinged dual seat and tool tray (1963-on); center & side stands.

**CONTROLS** Orthodox British layout.

**LIGHTING** 6v x 36w headlight (1963-on 12v x 45w headlight).

**DIMENSIONS** *Wheelbase* 55.5in. (1410mm); 1965-on: 55in. (1397mm). *Weight* 370lb. (168kg).

**SPEED** *Cruising* 77–87mph (124–140km/h). *Maximum* 112–117mph (180–188km/h).

**CONSUMPTION** 50–65mpg (5.6–4.3l/100km).

**POWER** 47bhp at 6700rpm.

**PRICE** (new UK, 1963) £322.

THE MID-1960S WERE momentous years for Triumph, but nothing exceeded in importance Edward Turner's retirement as MD at Meriden. His personal dislike of racing no longer held sway, so when his former second-in-command, Bert Hopwood, took over, the first thing he did was to persuade Dougle Hele, his old working partner from his Norton days, to leave Norton and join Triumph. Until then Hele's greatest achievement had been the development of the works Norton "Domiracer."

## Triumph at Daytona

In the U.S., plans were laid to end the Harley-Davidson-advantaged AMA regulation which permitted home-produced 750 cc side-valves to race against imported 500 cc overhead-valve bikes. The BSA group had a 750 Triple underway with which to meet the probable H.D. ohv 750 twin, but in the meantime it had to do the best it could with whatever was at hand. And that was the newish T100A unit-construction short-stroke 500. At Daytona Gary Nixon had come second on a race-prepared model in 1964. By 1966 the new racers were ready, developing between 45 and 46 bhp at 8200 rpm, although in practice they all blew up. But Hele persisted and Buddy Elmore eventually brought his T100A to victory. Nixon, also on a T100A, would have won but for a puncture toward the end of the race. Harley was speechless: Triumph was overjoyed. The following year, Triumph's Daytona victory over H.D. was even greater, because its much-improved T100 (approx. 50bhp) racers this time (Nixon and Elmore) not only won, but devastatingly lapped every other competitor.

In celebration Triumph launched a road-going "replica" of its racers: the great T100R Daytona. Now this basic engine had been around since the 5TA unit-construction Speed Twin of 1959 and in sports form since the T100A of a year later in

34bhp at 7000rpm format. Frankly it had been a disappointment compared to the earlier pre-unit T100, principally because the short-stroke engine lacked the older engine's excellent torque development, yet without any great power bonus. While Triumph failed thereafter to persuade any commendable low- or medium-engine-speed torque from its short-stroke 500, that which it

▼ THE GREAT PERCY TAIT, PERHAPS THE MOST DEDICATED TRIUMPH RIDER IN THE HISTORY OF THE FACTORY. HERE HE IS ON HIS QUITE INCREDIBLE RIDE IN THE BELGIAN GRAND PRIX AT SPA-FRANCORCHAMPS IN 1969.

▶ DON RICKMAN, WHO WITH BROTHER DEREK WAS A MOTO-CROSS ACE AND A SUPREME ROLLING-CHASSIS CONSTRUCTOR, RIDING ONE OF HIS OWN TRIUMPH ENGINED METTISE MACHINES AT THE BRITISH MX GRAND PRIX, IN 1966.

squeezed out of the same competition engines exceeded that of any other of its twins.

In 1967 Nixon lapped Daytona at 140.8mph (226.69km/h), which suggests a top speed of at least 150mph (242km/h). From a race-tuned roadster, whatever the cunning technology employed, it was incredible and quite the equal of the more glamorous Daytona Trident's accomplishments.

The roadster T100R Daytona was, as may be expected, not tuned to those standards, but it was certainly the quickest twin roadster Triumph had ever built. With a rider of average stature, dressed in a two-piece storm suit and crouching over the tank, one of these trim little twins would knock up something very close to 115mph (185km/h). If that same rider swapped the touring bars and footrests for clip-ons and rear-sets and exchanged his storm-suit for racing leathers, 120mph (193km/h) was awaiting him. In the hands of an experienced rider, one of these was faster than a Bonneville around a mountain road: it weighed a bare 330lb. (150kg), yet put 39bhp at its rider's whim.

## Supreme handling and road-holding

The old 5TA frame had been a thorough disgrace, but the Daytona was not simply a later one with a stronger steering head: it also enjoyed the end-plate-bolted swinging-fork pivot and much improved steering geometry, thanks to Hele's work. Handling and road-holding were pure magic.

In the best traditions of Triumph twins, the 5TA engine proved to be as adept at off-road competition as on it. It probably achieved its peak in 1966 when all the British ISDT team was equipped with versions of the engine, including a couple of 3TAs (the 350 cc brother). Roy Peplow and Sammy Miller used the 490 cc version, Ken Heanes an overbored 501 cc engine for the

unlimited class, and on the 350s were Ray Sayer and Johnny Giles. Unfortunately the East German team beat them by a handful of points, although Triumph won the manufacturers' award and all trophy team members won Gold Medals. Significantly another version of the 5TA first appeared in this event: the BSA Victor moto-cross framed model, as ridden by Arthur Lampkin. When the FIM nominated Massachusetts as the 1973 ISDT venue, the AMA went for the TR5T.

The machines were changed almost beyond recognition by Triumph in California, and the Americans surprised the world by winning the Vase award that year. The British, in a state of bemused delight, found themselves taking second place to the victorious Czechoslovakian team, in the prestigious Trophy contest on TR5T prepared to the same specification as the U.S. team by the same U.S. engineers.

Malcolm Rathmell on a T100A-powered Cheyney framed "Trophy" in the IoM-hosted ISDT of 1971.

The supersport roadster Daytona, inspired by Triumph's success with the US circuit. It was by far the quickest sportster of its period. Although a push rod engine, it would rev into double figures.

SPECIFICATION

# 500 T100R DAYTONA

**ENGINE** Air-cooled 360° parallel twin in unit with transmission. *Capacity* 490cc. *Bore & stroke* 69 x 65.5mm. *Compression ratio* 9:1. *Valves* 4 x ohv pushrod. *Carburation* twin Amal Monoblocs. *Lubrication* dry sump, gear pump. *Ignition* Lucas x 2 coil and c/b. *Crankcase* vertically split. *Crankshaft* one-piece forging, twin ball-race mains, split shell big-ends. *Generator* crankshaft AC. *Starting* kick.

**TRANSMISSION** *Primary drive* duplex chain. *Clutch* multiplate. *Gear selection* right-side foot lever. *Gear ratios* 1st, 14.09; 2nd, 9.18; 3rd, 6.95; 4th, 5.7:1.

**FRAME** All-welded single-loop duplex engine cradle.

**SUSPENSION** *Front* ex-BSA tele-fork with two-way damping. *Rear* swinging fork on Girling units.

**WHEELS** *Front* 3.25in. (82.6mm) tire on 18in. (457mm) rim. *Brake* 7in. (178mm) 2ls drum. *Rear* 3.5in. (89mm) tire on 18in. (457mm) rim. *Brake* 7in. (178mm) 1ls drum.

**EQUIPMENT** 3 gal. (13.6l) steel fuel tank; 5 pt. (2.8l) oil tank; rev counter; ignition- and oil-warning lights; tank-top carrier; center and side stands; steering lock; 12v 50w headlight.

**DIMENSIONS** *Wheelbase* 54.5in. (1384mm). *Weight* 360lb. (163.4kg).

**SPEED** *Cruising* 75–85mph (121–137km/h). *Maximum* 112–117mph (180–188km/h).

**CONSUMPTION** 55–70mpg (5.1–4l/100km).

**POWER** 39bhp at 7400–8000rpm.

**PRICE** (new UK) £331.

# 1969 750 T150 TRIDENT

SOMEONE WITH A wry sense of humor once observed that the mighty Vincent V-twins were prototypes that had gotten into production. The Trident, along with its BSA brother, the R75 Rocket Three, was much less radical, yet a similar comment might apply. In the 13-year life-span of the triples, although they were improved and modernized, they remained essentially old-fashioned motorcycles by virtue of their defiance of progressive production engineering. This is understandable when one appreciates that the design began on the project as long ago as 1961.

## Assembly problems

The 5T-based twin's great virtue was that it relied on the same basic constituents as a single – two crankcase halves only. The T150 engine consisted of five major layers of aluminum castings. Assembly of the bottom half demanded the most delicate alignment via countless jigs following over 50 boring and cutting operations. If this was not enough, because of their heritage, the engines required selected component assembly. Unless the twin necessities of micro-accurate engine assembly and meticulous component selection were observed, the Trident was doomed. Beyond that, a new engine required a protracted bedding-in procedure: it took the form of a constant measuring and torquing down of cylinder-head nuts and consequential partnering of valve-clearance adjustment over at least a 2,000-mile (3,220km) running time.

## Honda-crunching performance

Ironically, even a moderately well-prepared Trident could blow the socks off its great rival, the Honda CB750 Four. It would beat the glamorous Japanese in all dynamics, whether on road or race circuit, and so it continued until factory race efforts ceased in the early 1970s and roadster

TRIDENTS LACKED THE ASTONISHING ADAPTABILITY OF THEIR TWIN COUNTERPARTS, BUT THAT DIDN'T DAMPEN THE ENTHUSIASM OF SOME RIDERS. THIS IS A WASP MOTO-CROSS OUTFIT, SPONSORED BY KEN HEANES.

VETTER MADE THE MOST OF THE X75'S TRIPLE BUGLES. BSA CALLED ITS VERSION THE HURRICANE.

A SAD STORY IF EVER THERE WAS: THE CRAIG VETTER-STYLED X75. BSA ASKED VETTER FOR SOMETHING SPECIAL AND GOT IT – BUT THEN, ALLEGEDLY, FOUND SETTLEMENT A LITTLE DIFFICULT. THE X75'S STYLING WAS SO INSPIRATIONAL IT CHANGED THE SHAPE OF MOTORCYCLE DESIGN.

production of the T160 ceased in 1974. Unfortunately, by 1975 the BSA Group had introduced a "modern" production system, and the old selected-component assembly system had been discontinued in favor of a first-come-first-fitted production system using mainly non-craftsmen assembly workers. The inevitable result of such carelessness was predictable – although it was only one element in the BSA Group's final collapse.

The Trident's original engine dimensions were those of the T100 (63 x 80mm), but were quickly changed to 67 x 70mm in order to gain the improved valve angles and sizes vital to obtain the sort of power impossible with the "strangled" old T100. The production engine in most respects, was as different from the T100 as the T100 was from that which inspired it – the 1934 Mk 5 250 single. Perhaps its greatest strength was its unique crankshaft. Neither composite nor simple forging,

it was actually a very high-grade steel forging twisted into the three 120° throws. Bob-weights, as integral webs, at each journal took the place of a flywheel. Combined with the inherently good balance of the triple, it was a mighty tough bottom end.

## A modern classic

The fundamental soundness of the Trident may be gauged by the evidence of the standard crankshaft's use throughout the entire race history of the engine. The Daytona and F750 engines were developing between 85 and 86bhp, while modern overbored 1000s, still on the standard crankshaft, are developing 98bhp *at the rear wheel* with impunity.

◀ THE FINAL DEVELOPMENT OF THE TRIDENT WAS AS THE BSA SLOPER-ENGINED ELECTRIC STARTED T160. IT WAS A POTENTIALLY GREAT MACHINE, LET DOWN ONLY BY SLOPPY PRODUCTION QUALITY. NVT, WHICH HELD MARKETING RIGHTS BY THIS TIME, HAD FIRM PLANS FOR A 900CC VERSION.

A 1969 TRIDENT, COMPLETE WITH "DAN DARE" MUFFLERS, SLABBY STYLING, WIRE WHEELS, AND DRUM BRAKES. NEVERTHELESS, THESE VERY EARLY MODELS ARE CONSIDERED BY THE KNOWLEDGEABLE TO BE SOME OF THE BEST TO HAVE LEFT THE FACTORY BECAUSE OF THEIR HIGH PRODUCTION QUALITY.

## SPECIFICATION

# 1969 750 T150 TRIDENT

**ENGINE** Air-cooled 120° transverse in-line three in unit with gearbox. *Capacity* 740cc. *Bore & stroke* 67 x 70mm. *Compression ratio* 9.5:1. *Valves* 6 x ohv pushrod. *Carburation* 3 x 27mm Amal Monoblocs. *Lubrication* dry sump, gear pump. *Ignition* Lucas x 3 coil & c/b. *Crankcase* vertically split, twin central-bush-drive side-roller timing side ball-race mains, split shell plain big-ends. *Crankshaft* one-piece steel forging. *Generator* crankshaft AC. *Starting* kick.

**TRANSMISSION** *Primary drive* triplex chain. *Clutch* dry single plate diaphragm. *Gear selection* right-side foot lever. *Gear ratios* 1st, 12.8; 2nd, 8.9; 3rd, 6.5; 4th, 5.3:1.

**FRAME** All-welded single-loop duplex engine cradle.

**SUSPENSION** *Front* ex-BSA tele-fork with two-way damping. *Rear* swinging fork on Girling units.

**WHEELS** *Front and rear* 19in. (482mm). *Front* 4.10in. (104mm) tire. *Brake* 8in. (203mm) 2ls drum. *Rear* as front. *Brake* 7in. (178mm) drum.

**EQUIPMENT** Dual seat; 3.8 gal. (17.3l) steel fuel tank; tool kit; rev counter; oil & ignition warning lights; turn signals; center and side stands; steering lock.

**LIGHTING** 12v 50w headlight.

**DIMENSIONS** *Wheelbase* 57in. (1448mm). *Weight* 492lb. (223.4kg).

**SPEED** *Cruising* 90–100mph (145–161km/h). *Maximum* 118–126mph (190–203km/h).

**CONSUMPTION** 42–48mpg (6.7–5.9l/100km).

**POWER** 58bhp at 7500rpm.

**PRICE** (new UK) £614.

# STARTING OVER: TRIUMPH AT HINCKLEY

*T*he most remarkable thing about Triumph now is that it has been successfully resurrected. Its motorcycles are currently very different  from what they once were at Meriden in Turner's day. Then they were light, agile, and adaptable: now they are heavy, stable grand turismos of an entirely different ilk. There are signs (at the time of writing), however, that the new company at Hinckley in Leicestershire, England, is beginning to plow its own furrow. It is showing serious interest in exchanging top-end roadster power for middle-range torque and appears to be seriously investigating the possibility of racing in the foreseeable future.

THE MYSTERY MAN is John Bloor. By profession he is a large-scale property developer and builder of both commercial premises and private houses, usually as complete subdivisions. He rode a motorcycle as a young man, but has no particular enthusiasm for motorcycling as a personal hobby. Precisely why he ventured into a business in Britain that had become tainted with failure is unclear and, in the early stages, perhaps it was even to himself. He is, however, a cautious businessman who never makes a move without fully investigating his new marketplace first.

The precise truth about Bloor's original intentions regarding Triumph will probably remain unknown for years, but the tale has become part of motorcycling folklore and deserves repeating. When in 1983 Bloor became aware that the old Triumph factory was for sale, he saw its potential as a valuable site for property development. Only on attending the auction did he discover that everything was for sale, including all the rights in the Triumph name. To his great surprise, the name and associated rights were plainly considered by those present to be worth very little. On realizing that he could lose very little if his "nose" for what seemed a bargain proved wrong, he bid, and found himself the owner of a proud old ghost.

Apart for a few rumors, nothing more was heard about John Bloor and Triumph for a few years. Just before the cooperative company's collapse in 1981, it had announced a dummy model of a proposed machine called the Phoenix, a water-cooled 900 cc ohc twin of modular concept which, by means of stroke changes, was suitable for one- or three-cylinder construction in 500 and 1200 cc sizes. Weary of empty rumor, the motorcycling world grinned wryly and said nowt.

Quite suddenly and unexpectedly in 1988, the industry became aware of the erection of a brand new, if compact, and plainly very business-like motorcycle factory. The location was Hinckley,

Leicestershire, and the builder, not surprisingly, was Bloor's own company. A press release revealed that the premises would house the wherewithal to manufacture a wholly new line of Triumphs entirely unrelated to the Meriden models, and that a team of engineers was already fully employed on design and development. What little information was released about them made it plain that any relationship to the Phoenix existed only in the imagination.

The British motorcycle press was in turns delighted at the news, intrigued by the project, and outraged by the secrecy surrounding it. Hinckley was shut tighter than a drum. It was typical of Bloor. No one who did not need to know would know anything until Bloor chose to tell them. The press fumed: Hinckley worked on.

## The new way forward

Up to this time, although an often contentious relationship existed between the motorcycle press and the old industry, the passage of information between the two was excellent. The individuals within the two spheres either knew each other personally or by reputation. Hinckley Triumph, however, was an alien. The mystery to journalists whose principal interest was, understandably, technological, was the identities of these unknown new engineers and their track records. Bloor had decided from the start that his would be a company without the cult of premium personalities. His engineers were simply the best he could find, drawn from industries as apparently remote as the railroad and as close as the car. Such a design team would have been impossible as recently as the 1970s (as Eric Turner and Lionel Jofeh found to their eternal discredit), when knowledge of the essentials of good motorcycle design was the exclusive property of a small number of specialist motorcycle engineers alone. By the 1980s the old rule-of-thumb methods had

been made obsolete by the huge amount of scientific research that had been carried out into all aspects of motorcycle design and behavior, and made public via innumerable papers from both industry and academia. And it was locked into the electronic ganglia of computers rather than the transient receptacles of the human mind.

To an extent perhaps greater than in any other high-profile industry, Bloor was teaching the British lessons they should have learned more than two decades before: empiricism in engineering design was finished, and the most important engineers now lay with production, not design. Precisely *who* these folk were was an irrelevance, of course.

The remarkable thing was that, unlike, say, Rover cars, which had recently undergone the metamorphosis from old-world manual piecemeal assembly to fully integrated computerized production, Triumph at Hinckley appeared to be the progeny of virgin birth. One year there had been a green field, the next a motorcycle production facility of the most advanced type. It went against the grain of all, or at least most, western European advice and forecasts for the foreseeable future: motorcycle manufacturing was the business of nations in the second phase of industrial development, following bicycles. The evidence was there for all to see: witness the virtual collapse of almost the entire European motorcycle industry in the 1960s, not merely Britain's. That, at least, was the opinion of the City of London's financial experts, with the tragedy of Hesketh's V-twin still vivid in the memory.

The matter of the capitalization of Triumph has intrigued a multitude of pundits. Most that has been publicly circulated is conjecture. Capitalization sums of anything between £40 million and £80 million ($60–120 million) have been bandied about. The only certain knowledge is that, whatever the size of the investment, none of it came from British banks; in all probability its source is Bloor himself.

## Launching the new breed

Wisely, Bloor made the decision to launch his new Triumphs not in their home country, but at one of the world's two great international motorcycle shows, Cologne, Germany in 1990 (the other being Milan, Italy). British pragmatism, one of the UK's finest national characteristics, had during the decline of the old hot-metal industries turned to cynicism, even self-loathing. By displaying abroad what for Europe in general and Britain in particular was a selection of disconcertingly familiar machines of plainly Japanese influence to continental Europeans, Bloor neatly sidestepped the possibly acerbic reaction of British motorcycle journalists. Further, Triumph's publicity department wooed not the specialist motorcycle press, but the international general media. It was a masterstroke. With a marveling, congratulatory world on its side, Triumph had won the first round hands down.

Bloor's other great victory was the winning of the motorcycle retail trade's trust. Triumph Meriden had finally crumbled in a welter of scorn and hatred from dealers who could no longer withstand the ever-increasing torrent of warranty claims. They turned for their bread-and-butter to other suppliers, usually Japanese, whose products, once sold, rarely returned with factory-originated troubles. To a degree exceeding even that of the press, the wounded retail trade was deeply suspicious. Even before the Cologne launch, Bloor had set up the foundation of a new dealer network. These shrewd businessmen were impressed, not simply with the material quality of the motorcycles themselves, but with the high quality of the service they experienced from Bloor's men. Triumph had won the second round.

## Brand loyalty: the old and the new

The third round was no easier. Loyalty to the old brand name was still, among a powerfully influential minority, very strong. It appears to have surprised even Bloor, who from the outset made a point of disassociating Triumph Hinckley from Triumph Meriden, as manifested in the subtle but significant change in the Triumph logo. Hinckley began to discover by degrees that it was, if not quite peering into the abyss, then it was at least looking at a murky ditch. It simply could not trade on the old glory without a recognizable acquaintanceship. Since early 1994, a definite softening of attitude toward its obsolete forebears and the dedicated bands of enthusiasts who

support the old brand has become apparent.

When the new factory was completed in 1990, it occupied an 11-acre site. Since then it has expanded, and when complete the new extended plant will cover 48 acres. By the end of 1992 – the first full year of production – 4,900 motorcycles had been manufactured. By the end of 1993, 8,000 had left the factory, and at the start of business

1995, 12,000 models had rolled out of the gates. Astonishingly, by this time all the 1995 production had been sold to the trade!

During 1994 an American sales network was set up, to be administered from a Triumph-owned subsidiary, Triumph Motorcycles America Ltd., in Peachtree City, Atlanta, Georgia. The company has two other subsidiaries in France and Germany.

# HINCKLEY: THE MOTORCYCLES

TODAY, IN MOST high-tech industries, you do not tackle the Japanese head-on and live to tell the tale. In motorcycling tradition, the V twin is American, the flat twin is German, and the parallel twin is British. The Italian motorcycle? The Italians, thankfully, are a race still in creative-thrall to the spirit of the Rennaisance and contradict all attempts to typecast. But Japan has made the transverse-four its own. The world knows it is so. Yet Bloor's Triumph, so small its bravura amounted to mere impudence, elected to build a British motorcycle that broke the mold: it looks like a Japanese motorcycle, it sounds like a Japanese motorcycle, and it performs like a Japanese motorcycle – superficially.

## Component sources

Suspension performance was excellent in all respects, as was braking and lighting. As these vital auxiliaries are all bought in, rather than manufactured in-house, it is scarcely surprising. Triumph's long-term plan is to produce as many of its parts itself as possible. It already has machine facilities and chassis fabrication operations to compare with the world's best elsewhere, and these are continually expanding to maximize manufacturing possibilities. This is unlikely to involve electrical, braking, and suspension systems simply because of the highly specialized knowledge and skills required. At the time of writing, brakes, suspension, and electrical generator are Japanese, simply because they are the best, and supplies are sourced from companies familiar with the modern requirement of continuous supply rather than the old-style bulk annual order. Reviews are always in

▶ FOR HARLEY DAVIDSON, THE NIGHTMARE RETURNS IN THE FORM OF ITS OLD ADVERSARY'S NEW THUNDERBIRD.

hand with alternatives, and at the time of writing serious consideration was being paid to Italian suspension suppliers. The ignition system is German.

Ironically, if unsurprisingly, most of Triumph's production machinery is Japanese. The story goes that John Bloor visited some Japanese factories and, on learning that Yamaha had the most advanced cylinder-head machining operation, sought out the manufacturer of the plant concerned and ordered the same. This may well account for the adoption of valve-shimming assembles identical in most part to certain Yamaha models. The whole operation is computer controlled: raw, blank cylinder-head castings are fed into the machine at one end and the finished head exits from the other.

## Engines: the new technology

There appears to be a strong similarity of design between the Kawasaki GPZ900, top end especially, and Triumph engines. This has led to all manner of speculation, even to the suggestion of Kawasaki investment in Triumph. From the reaction of senior Triumph management, this would appear to be very far from the truth. Every designer plumbs the inbuilt knowledge of his competitors' engines by bench testing and then dissecting the most promising units. It would be wasteful not to, because it is the practical shortcut to progress. Even had Triumph designers "simply" copied – as they did not – another engine, in the long term the exercise would have lacked commercial

viability because of Triumph engineers' lack of foundation technology on which to build.

An answer to the riddle of Triumph engine's origins is to be found in a paper published by the Society of Engineers (SAE) for the International Congress and Exposition held at Detroit, Michigan, in February 1991. The authors were Anthony V. Smith, an engineer of Ricardo Consulting Engineers, Sussex, England, and S. G. Stewart, an engineer at Triumph (Designs) Ltd., Hinckley. Their paper's title was "The Design of Lightweight Reciprocating Components for a New Family of High-Speed Motorcycle Engines." It makes fascinating, and revealing, reading and, incidentally, has linked Triumph once more to Ricardo, which was responsible for the old 500 cc four-valve single of 1921. Too few people are aware of Ricardo, whose philosophy until comparatively recently was to allow its clients to enjoy public acclaim for whatever products they themselves had developed. Ricardo is probably the world's foremost independent design and development company in the internal combustion-based manufacturing industry. With the exception of Mercedes, Yamaha, and a very few others, Ricardo is either responsible for, or has had a hand in, the design and/or development of vehicles, particularly engines, for most of the world's makers.

Regarding the origins of the Triumph engine, Smith and Stewart's paper had this to say: "The approach [previously] described enabled a competitive lightweight design of piston, [gudgeon] pin and connecting rod to be produced on a 'right-first-time' basis as part of a single stage design and development programme. Sufficient confidence as placed in the approach for production rather than prototype tooling to be procured on the basis of the analytical results. Subsequent testing was carried out on entirely production parts." And a later paragraph: "Advances in predictive analysis techniques have largely enabled . . . the elimination at the design stage of problems that would have traditionally been resolved within the framework of [an extensive] development test programme." And further on: "In the case of the new family of

Triumph motorcycle engines, the philosophy of right-first-time design was applied in the extreme for the design of the reciprocating components."

In other words, Ricardo was going to present Triumph with its engine's most highly stressed

components which would meet all requirements without time-consuming and costly development. For the first time in Britain, at least, an engine would be built according to truly scientific methods, rather than the traditional protracted and

often seriously flawed suck-it-and-see empirical system. From this it can be concluded that the Triumph engine is an original, and that its appearance in such short time was a consequence of applied science rather than sneakery or luck. It is safe to assume that with the huge volume of information now available about chassis design, a similar approach to success was employed there as well.

## Modular-design concept

Bert Hopwood must be grinning from ear to ear, if a little ruefully: as soon as he took over the old BSA/Triumph duo from Edward Turner in 1964, he proposed the adoption of a modular design concept and advanced production techniques, which of course was rejected by the board. The motorcycles built at Hinckley probably represent, at least at the top end of the scale, what he had in mind. The current line consists of 11 models varying in size through 750, 900, and 1200 cc. Most models are available in various engine sizes and styles (though the 750 is available only as the Trident 750). They all share an identical rolling chassis, transmission system, and engine castings. Variations occur between models in such particulars as suspension-spring strengths, rear-wheel sprocket sizes, exhaust systems, bodywork panels, seats and instrumentation, but otherwise they have a great deal in common.

What's more, Triumph plans to keep it this way, confident that its engine has a great deal of development (or, rather, planned future design) left in it for many years yet. The advantage is that it keeps down costs, simplifies spares and service facilities, and provides the sort of continuity the mercurial Japanese-reliant dealers must dream about.

With the exception of the rear-suspension swinging fork, in aluminum alloy, the frame is nothing more than a spine fabricated from high-grade tensile steel. The massive block of the power

unit is the principal load bearer.

By an ironic twist of fate, the crankshafts are German-made to a process pioneered by Triumph Meriden for the old Trident. They are forged with the big-end journals in line and then hot-twisted to their designed throw before machining. Most of the rest of the engine is British-made, with a great deal of both development technology and actual castings from the famous Cosworth company. It could be done more cheaply, but the new Triumphs do not conform to the familiar minimalist construction of so many big bike engines but are, by general consensus, handsomely over-engineered. Such a policy provides great strength now and for future development. Weight could be saved, but only at serious cost to longevity. Significantly, experienced mechanics are of the opinion that Triumph engines are easier to work on than most of their type, finding greater simplicity and more room.

The soundness of such a policy is reflected in the general demeanor of the line. The Sprint 900, for instance, manifested subtle yet insistent signals of a solidity unusual among its type. No one has phrased it better than *Motor Cycle International*, a British magazine with a mature perspective on motorcycling: "Their [Triumph's] build quality is terrific. They are built to please Germans." The truth of this is revealed in the average age of new Triumph buyers: 39 years old. By then a motorcyclist has become discriminating.

## The sporting side

One model does not conform to the general line's performance: the Daytona 1200s and Super 111 (900) are undisguised sportsters offering the kind of speed potential to compete directly with the top Japanese sportsters, such as the Suzuki GSXR1100. The 1200 develops a staggering 145bhp (147PS) at 9500rpm. At 4.484:1, it is geared for an ideal top speed of 150mph (242km/h); this it exceeds with ease, clearing over 155mph (250km/h) and, when conditions allow, nudging 160mph (258km/h). The remarkable thing is that the Triumph frame and suspension are still capable of taming the beast. Fast it may be, but the consensus of opinion is that the 900 cc Daytona 111 is even quicker! The much less massive build of the triple gives it an edge, although to deal with such speeds, its pure racing brakes incorporate six pistons per caliper (12 per front wheel!) and demand the skills of the most experienced to manage safely. The Daytona is largely a product of Cosworth race engineering, which redeveloped and then specially manufactured the standard cylinder head to racing standards.

## Development potential

Even though they are founded on Ricardo's "right-first-time" scientific principle, and allowing for their very brief production span of four years, the new Trumpets still offer considerable scope for development. The first new basic engine was the 750, sporting a bore and stroke of 75 x 55mm. It was quadrupled into the 1000 four (998 cc), as exemplified by the Daytona 1000 sportster released in 1992. Triumph was still feeling its way, but it seemed that this "short-stroke" engine would become the prestige sportster unit. Already, however, the "long-stroke" 900 (885 cc) triples were attracting much greater interest among public, trade, and press, largely because of their unique combination of high torque, high power, exemplary handling, and singularly compulsive personality. Hinckley was unwilling to alter its precious combustion-chamber format to achieve

new engine capacities, so in 1993 the old "short-stroke" 1000 four was dropped and development of new prestige sportsters given to Cosworth; these were to be based on the popular "long-stroke" triple and 1200 (1180 cc) four, which continued to share their common 75mm bore, but had grown in stroke to 65mm. The Trident 750, which retains the shorter-stroked engine, is a very underrated machine. It is noticeably smoother than its bigger brothers and, while lacking their monstrous mid-range torque, its engine's responsiveness to the throttle is electrifying, especially above 7000rpm – where the difference in power output between it and a 900 is hardly noticeable in practice.

Fascinatingly, the original Daytona 1000 models have already become modern classics, objects of high desire among collectors.

## Riding the Sprint 900

The Sprint 900 is Britain's most popular new Triumph. It is styled centrally between the fully faired Trophy 900 and the naked Speed Triple, but shares an identical power unit and practically identical rolling chassis construction. By far the majority of enthusiasts these days cut their motorcycling teeth on Japanese motorcycles. In consequence an awful lot of them feel uncomfortable dealing with what they regard as the quirky characteristics of machinery not of this

▶ TRIUMPH'S ELITE GRAN' TOURISMO, THE TROPHY 1200. ITS FORMIDABLE TOP HAMPER IS TOO MUCH FOR HILL ROAD SCRATCHING, BUT AS AN AUTOBAHN BURNER, IT IS BULLET PROOF.

ilk. Like most other enthusiasts, motorcyclists in general wish to take their stamp of individuality only far enough to distinguish them from the world at large – but not so far as to separate them from their kindred spirits. So Triumph has provided a motorcycle that conforms in all major areas with what has become motorcycling's (Asian) norm, yet which is immediately identifiable as intriguingly different.

When the Sprint 900 was fired up, it did so with that familiar singing *whirr* and it idled reliably with the light metallic *frou-frou* of all modern, water-cooled, twin-cam multis. The clutch was light, the gears meshed effortlessly, and its whole demeanor encouraged an easy slide into city traffic streams with the confidence of complete controllability. Blinker, horn, and light switches were all in their accustomed place and could be used with unconscious ease. The sophistication of what amounted to an almost brand-new motorcycle – or as brand new as few are these days – belied its brief production life and implied long years of painstaking development.

The bike was quiet, flexible, wholly undemanding, and without evidence of those odd personality traits that are supposed to be the stuff of strong individuality. But herein lay the danger. After 30 minutes of riding, the impression grew that here was the blandly rolling headstone of the grave of the "authentic" Triumphs. During the next 30 minutes, however, subtle nuances of a deeper personality began to impress, the most profound of which was the power delivery. Regardless of how thoughtlessly the twistgrip was snatched back at ultra-low revs, without hiccup or hesitation the engine growled a little as with growing strength it accelerated the machine forward, quickly turning civility into shrieking fury, and the rider's desperate wish for a more effective back-stop!

In top gear alone, the Sprint 900's rider can expect a speed *range* of 107mph (172km/h), covering an engine-speed band of 7150rpm. In practice it can, with a little sensitivity, be stretched to the point where in top gear both rev counter and speedometer needles are barely moving; but such stunts are impractical.

Only a fool would dispute Japan's claim to some of the world's finest engineers. With rare exceptions, though, they seem to be incapable or unwilling to incorporate the right sort of torque development into their engines. In this respect their singles are a disgrace. It is reflected in the power characteristics of their fours, which can deliver smooth, low-speed torque, but usually lack the necessary muscle at low revs. Or, if it is present, it is only in partnership with ponderous tourers handling of the great mass that seems obligatory with Japanese. The Sprint 900 was, in the best sense, an all-rounder, combining speed and civility.

## Delivering the power

Ah, civility! Well, yes, but . . . up to 3000 and 4000rpm, which roughly equates to 53mph (85km/h) in top gear, the engine's power delivery could be compared with that of an old SU-carburated Thunderbird – liquid and lovely. From thereon the big triple got down to business and began to accelerate hard and fast. This continued until, at a little over 7000rpm and 106mph (170km/h) in top gear, it really climbed on the cam. Acceleration in the intermediate gears from these revs was simply stupendous, and power applications required deliberation if they were not to get out of hand. Even in top gear, acceleration up to 120mph (193km/h) was of the type that raises bold, bad grins. Top speed appeared to be at least 130mph (209km/h). It goes without saying that quick cog-swaps needed no reference to the clutch, either up or down the transmission. Frankly, six speeds could have been adopted only as a marketing ploy: in practice, five, or even four, would have been ample.

## Handling and comfort

A great deal of emphasis these days is placed on handling; perhaps rightly so because its two partnering dynamics – roadholding and stability – are currently almost without exception so unerringly correct they are taken as read. As a consequence the minutiae of a fast bike's reaction to high-speed direction changing has become paramount, even though it may contribute little to the total on-road performance of the motorcycle. What once was a quantifiable dynamic has become a matter of perception: no longer what it does, but the way it does it – molecularly. Possibly the Sprint 900 is a little heavier to handle in extremis than some, but at the velocities required to positively identify it, such business has become somewhat academic and certainly beyond the pale on public roads.

Curiously enough vibration, the ruinous and discomforting gremlin of old Triumph, and which was also measurable, has also become subjective. Some, mainly younger, riders have criticized the current line of Triumph triples as vibratory. The Sprint 900's engine could be felt working, and rightly so; but not even at its highest revs did it tingle or buzz and, combined with the engine's huge torque spread, its lightly sensed "rumblegutz" nature was one of its great attractions. The all-too common ailment of high-frequency zuzz-numbed fingers among modern big-multi riders was absent.

The only fault worth noting was the unavoidable and wearying turbulence eddying and vortexing over the low sports windshield. It buffeted around the head like an invisible, flapping sheet. Admittedly, motorcycle designers have their hands full in a way unknown to their four-wheeler counterparts in coping with the aerodynamics of perpendicular axes. But these have been public knowledge since BMW's pioneering R100 RS of 1977. It is inconceivable that Triumph knows no better by this time.

# SPRINT 900

This model forms the basic specification of all the new Triumphs. Variations to this common format are itemized separately.

**ENGINE** Water-cooled transverse parallel three in unit with transmission. *Capacity* 885 cc. *Bore & stroke* 76 x 65mm. *Compression ratio* 10.6:1 *Valves* 12 x chain dohc. *Carburation* 3 x 36mm Mikuni CV. *Lubrication* wet sump, gear pump; some transmission components pressure fed. *Ignition* electronic. *Crankcase* horizontally split. *Crankshaft* one-piece "twist aligned" forging, 3 x 120° throw, 5 plain mains, split-shell big-ends. *Electrics* 12 v over-transmission alternator. *Starting* electric.

**TRANSMISSION** *Primary drive gear* 1.75:1 reduction. *Transmission* chain. *Gear selection* left-side foot lever. *Gear ratios* overall 1st, 12.91; 2nd, 9.91; 3rd, 7.30; 4th, 6.09; 5th, 5.45; 6th, 5.07:1; final drive reduction 2.5:1 (45/18). *Clutch* wet multiplate, hydraulic.

**FRAME** Engine main stress member. Lightweight fabricated steel spine.

**SUSPENSION** *Front* Kayaba tele-fork with variable rate springs and rebound damping. *Rear* cast aluminum swinging fork via rising-rate rebound-damped single adjustable Kayaba unit.

**WHEELS** *Front* cast aluminum 17in. (432mm) x 3.5in. (89mm) rim. *Tire* tubeless 120/70ZR17. *Brake* 2 x 310mm floating disks & 2 x 4 calipers. *Rear* as above, but 18in. (457mm) x 4.5in. (114mm) Tire 160/60ZR18. *Brake* 1 x 255mm disk, 1 x 2 caliper.

**EQUIPMENT** 5.5gal. (25l) fuel tank; rev counter; twin mirrors; grease-sealed chain; eccentric spindle block chain adjusters; center and side stands. half fairing; adjustable handlebars; temperature & fuel guages.

**LIGHTING** 12v x 65w quartz-halogen headlight; turn signals.

**CONTROLS** Standard international layout.

**DIMENSIONS** *Wheelbase* 58.5in. (1486mm). *Weight* (fully equipped) 503lb. (228kg).

**POWER** 96bhp (98PS) at 9000rpm; torque 112lb/ft (83Nm) at 6500rpm.

**CONSUMPTION** 40–50mpg (7.06–5.6l/100km).

**SPEED** *Cruising* 100mph (161km/h)+. *Maximum* 130mph (209km/h)+.

# 900 TIGER (T9)

**ENGINE** *Compression* (Tb) 10.1.

**TRANSMISSION** *Gear ratios overall* 1st, 11.95: 2nd, 8.51: 3rd, 6.75: 4th, 5.64: 5th, 5.04:1 (Tb).

**WHEELS** *(T9) Front* wire-spoked 19in. (483mm) x 2.5in. (64mm) rim. *Tire* tubed 110/80, street/enduro. *Brake* 2 x 10.8in. (276mm) floating disks, 2 x 2 calipers. *Rear* wire-spoked 17in (432mm) x 3in. (76mm) rim. *Tire* tubed 140/80. *Brake* 255mm disk 1 x 2 caliper T9. (TB) *Front* 18in. (457mm) x 2.5in (64mm) rim. *Tire* 110/80 tubed. *Brake* single 12.6in. (320mm) disk, 1 x 2 caliper. *Rear* 3in. (76mm) rim. *Tire* 160/80 tubed tire. *Brake* 11in. (285mm) single disk, 1 x 2 caliper.

**DIMENSIONS** *Weight* fully equipped (T9) 490lb. (222.5kg); (TB) 515lb. (234kg).

**EQUIPMENT** *Petrol tank* (TB) 3.3gal. (15l).

**POWER** (T9) 84bhp (85PS) at 8000rpm; torque 111lb/ft (82Nm) at 6000rpm. (TB) 69bhp (70PS) at 8000rpm; torque 98lb/ft (72Nm) at 4800rpm.

**SPEED** *Maximum* (T9) 130mph (209km/h); (TB) 115mph (185km/h).

## THUNDERBIRD (TB)

**ENGINE** *Compression* (Tb) 10.1.

**TRANSMISSION** *Gear ratios overall* 1st, 11.95: 2nd, 8.51: 3rd, 6.75: 4th, 5.64: 5th, 5.04:1 (Tb).

**WHEELS** *(T9) Front* wire-spoked 19in. (483mm) x 2.5in. (64mm) rim. *Tire* tubed 110/80, street/enduro. *Brake* 2 x 10.8in. (276mm) floating disks, 2 x 2 calipers. *Rear* wire-spoked 17in. (432mm) x 3in. (76mm) rim. *Tire* tubed 140/80. *Brake* 255mm disk 1 x 2 caliper T9. (TB) *Front* 18in. (457mm) x 2.5in. (64mm) rim. *Tire* 110/80 tubed. *Brake* single 12.6in. (320mm) disk, 1 x 2 caliper. *Rear* 3in. (76mm) rim. *Tire* 160/80 tubed tire. *Brake* 11in. (285mm) single disk, 1 x 2 caliper.

**DIMENSIONS** *Weight* fully equipped (T9) 490lb. (222.5kg); (TB) 515lb. (234kg).

**EQUIPMENT** *Petrol tank* (TB) 3.3gal. (15l).

**POWER** (T9) 84bhp (85PS) at 8000rpm; torque 111lb/ft (82Nm) at 6000rpm. (TB) 69bhp (70PS) at 8000rpm; torque 98lb/ft (72Nm) at 4800rpm.

**SPEED** *Maximum* (T9) 130mph (209km/h); (TB) 115mph (185km/h).

# TRIDENT 750

**ENGINE** *Compression* 11:1.

**TRANSMISSION** *Gear ratios overall* 1st, 13.39; 2nd, 9.54; 3rd, 7.57; 4th, 6.32; 5th, 5.65; 6th, 5.26:1; final drive reduction 2.8:1 (48/17).

**WHEELS** As Sprint 900.

**POWER** 89bhp (90PS) at 10,000rpm: torque 92lb/ft (68Nm) at 8700rpm.

## DAYTONA SUPER 111

**ENGINE** *Compression* 12:1.

**POWER** 113bhp (115PS) at 9500rpm: torque 120lb/ft (89Nm) at 8500rpm.

**SPEED** 147mph (237km/h).

# INDEX

## PICTURE CREDITS AND ACKNOWLEDGMENTS

**6** John Gola; **7** Triumph Motorcycles; **8–9** National Motorcycle Museum (NMM); **10** David Minton; **11** EMAP Archives; **12** NMM; **13** EMAP; **14–15** EMAP; **16** NMM; **17** B R Nicholls; **18** NMM; **20** t EMAP, b NMM; **21** l EMAP, r EMAP, b NMM; **22–23** EMAP; **24** l B R Nicholls, r EMAP; **25** EMAP; **26** NMM; **27** EMAP; **28** t David Minton, b NMM; **29** t David Minton, b EMAP; **30–31** EMAP; **32** NMM; **33** t B R Nicholls, b Dan Mahony; **34** John Gola: **35** t; NMM, b Dan Mahony; **36–37** NMM; **38–39** NMM; **40** l EMAP, r NMM; **41** NMM; **42–43** EMAP; **44–45** NMM; **46–47** EMAP; **48** t, b NMM, r EMAP; **49** NMM; **50–51** EMAP; **52** t, b; NMM, l EMAP; **53** B R Nicholls; **54–55** NMM; **56** t NMM, b EMAP; **57** l B R Nicholls, r EMAP; **58–59** NMM; **60** David Minton; **61** EMAP; **62–63** EMAP; **64–65** EMAP; **66** NMM; **67** B R Nicholls; **68–69** NMM; **70** B R Nicholls; **71** B R Nicholls; **72** B R Nicholls; **73** EMAP; **74** t B R Nicholls, b NMM; **75** NMM; **76–77** NMM; **78–93** Triumph Motorcycles.

Quintet Publishing would like to thank the National Motorcycle Museum, Birmingham, for allowing us access to the collection for photography, and special thanks to John for helping move the bikes around (NMM pictures © Quintet Publishing Limited); also thanks to Carl Rossner for loaning bikes for photography and to Triumph Motorcycles. Index by Sheila Seacroft.